Lawfully Wedded Husband

LIVING OUT

Gay and Lesbian Autobiographies

David Bergman, Joan Larkin, and Raphael Kadushin
SERIES EDITORS

Lawfully Wedded Husband

How My Gay Marriage Will Save the American Family

Joel Derfner

The University of Wisconsin Press

The University of Wisconsin Press
1930 Monroe Street, 3rd Floor
Madison, Wisconsin 53711-2059
uwpress.wisc.edu

Printed in the United States of America

Library of Congress Cataloging-in-Publication Data
Derfner, Joel, author.
Lawfully wedded husband: how my gay marriage will save
the American family / Joel Derfner.
pages   cm — (Living out: gay and lesbian autobiographies)
ISBN 978-0-299-29490-8 (cloth: alk. paper)
ISBN 978-0-299-29493-9 (e-book)
1. Derfner, Joel.   2. Gay men—United States—Biography.
3. Gay authors—United States—Biography.
4. Same-sex marriage—United States.
I. Title.   II. Series: Living out.
PS3604.E754Z46   2013
811'.6—dc23
[B]
2013015044

for
my father

Contents

Lawfully Wedded Husband

Introduction

What are you guys wearing tomorrow?" asked the assistant director of *Girls Who Like Boys Who Like Boys*, the reality show my fiancé, Mike, and I were being filmed for in May of 2010.

"I'm wearing jeans and a nice vest," I said, "and Mike will be in shorts and a T-shirt."

There was a brief silence on the other end of the line. "Joel," the assistant director said, "this Iowa wedding is the culmination of your story arc."

"Right."

"If you're not dressed up, people will think you're not taking it seriously."

"Look," I said. "I promised Mike that this would be as low-key an event as we could possibly manage, and I've already broken that promise in more ways than I can count. Not dressing up is the one shred of evidence left that I actually care about his feelings."

"This is bad," the assistant director said, and waited.

"Okay," I said finally. "I'll talk to him about it."

"Great," said the assistant director. "It'll really help the audience understand what a special thing you're doing." I put my cell phone in my pocket, went back to the table at the restaurant where Mike and I were having lunch with his cousin DJ and DJ's boyfriend, Kevin, and promptly did not talk to him about it, because Mike's fury was already just shy of the boiling point, and the last thing I needed was for it to get any hotter less than twenty-four hours before our nuptials.

But then the assistant director called back, and then he called back again. In total he called *four times* during a one-hour lunch to ask about what we'd decided. At some point I realized he wasn't going to stop, so, bracing myself, I said, very gently, "Mike, the TV people called and they want to know, what would you think about . . . picking up some slacks, maybe?" Mike stared at me in silence. "And, um, a nice shirt?" I could practically feel the waves of rage emanating from him.

"Oh, fine," he sighed at last. "I need a new suit anyway."

The next morning, Mike looking spiffy in his new suit, we drove with DJ and Kevin from their place in Rochester, Minnesota, to Mike's hometown of Cedar Rapids, Iowa, one of only three states in the union at the time where two men could legally marry each other, met my father, my stepmother, Mike's mother, and my brother at the magistrate's office, and headed in.

After an attempt on my part, not remotely convincing, to feign surprise that my friend Sarah was waiting inside—the reality show was about the friendships between straight women and gay men, and she and I had both been forced to discuss on camera *ad nauseam* our disappointment that she wouldn't be at the wedding, but of course I'd known all along that she would—the magistrate told me and Mike to hold hands.

"Joel, repeat after me," he said. "I take you, Michael, to be my spouse, to have and to hold, from this day forward, to love, honor, and cherish, to comfort and respect, in sorrow and in joy, as long as we both shall live." I repeated after him, and then he went through it again with Mike. Once we were finished, he said, "And now, forasmuch as you have made your vows, each to the other, I pronounce you—"

But I suppose I really ought to start from the beginning.

1

Saying Yes

I bought more ornaments for the Christmas tree!" Mike called as he closed the front door behind him.

"We already have too many ornaments for the Christmas tree," I said, not looking up from *Persuasion*. Louisa was about to get her concussion, and I'd be damned if I was going to interrupt the story now just because my boyfriend had passed a store with shiny things in the window.

"I know, but these were so fabulous I couldn't help myself. Come and take a look at them."

"But I'm reading."

"Too bad. You have to come look at ornaments."

"Fine," I snapped, dog-earing the page—Captain Wentworth was unlikely to have a change of heart while I wasn't looking— and walked into the living room, where Mike stood beside the Christmas tree taking things out of shopping bags. (I'm Jewish, but Mike is not, so I seize the holiday as an opportunity to decorate.) I sat down on the couch, picked up the nearest bundle of pink tissue paper on the coffee table, and unwrapped it to find a huge, glittering purple star. "Oh, my God," I said; I could tell Mike was manipulating me by playing on my weakness for purple, but I was powerless to resist. "You're right. That's gorgeous."

"See?"

Perhaps this was worth a few minutes before returning to my book after all. I unwrapped another ornament, which revealed itself to be a shiny tin ear of corn.

"Hmph," I said. Mike is from Iowa and thinks of himself, because it drives me crazy, as a corn proselyte. He feels he has both the right and the responsibility to torment me by threatening to replace our chandelier with a corn-shaped light fixture or buying shiny tin ears of corn with which to titivate our Christmas tree. It's awful, but I haven't figured out yet how to stop him.

I unwrapped a couple more ornaments, which were, I was grateful to see, closer to the purple star than to the ear of corn. The contents of the last box, however, when I got it open, looked, confusingly, not like an ornament but like a ring sort of thing. It was round and heavy and gold, with an engraved pattern and a little pink jewel—lovely, but far too small to be a Christmas tree ornament. I turned to Mike, puzzled, and saw that he was down on one knee.

"Joel," he said, "will you marry me?"

And I looked at him, looked at the man who had been my comfort and my support for years, through trials and tribulations greater than I had ever expected to face, gazed deep into his eyes, so full of love, and said, "Hang on a second."

"What?"

"I'll be right back."

"Where are you going?" he asked.

"Okay," I answered, "I haven't been an astrology addict for years and years but this is super-extra important so I have to go check and make sure the moon isn't void of course. Stay right there."

I leapt over the coffee table, ran into Mike's office, prayed as I woke his computer up that the Cablevision gods might choose to be merciful today and allow us the elusive Internet access for which we so grossly overpaid their earthly representatives, checked the void-of-course ephemeris online, ran back, leapt over the coffee table again, turned to Mike, took his hands, and said, "Yes! Yes, I'll marry you!"

"I don't know, you left me hanging a long time. I've been having second thoughts."

"Get away from me."

"Your shirt is on inside out."

The ring was a little big; when I pointed out that we'd need to have it resized, though, Mike furrowed his brow. "I don't understand. I used one of your rings as a guide."

"Which one?"

"The one on the chain in your desk drawer."

"Are you serious?"

"Yes."

"Honey, that ring is a replica I bought online of the One Ring from *The Lord of the Rings*. That's the only size it comes in—they sell it with the chain because you're not supposed to wear it. Didn't you see all the Elvish lettering?"

"I've always *thought* you were the greatest force for evil in the world."

But we spent the evening watching romantic comedies with his arms around me all the same.

At this point, in 2007, Mike and I had been together for about four years; we'd known each other for a couple of years longer than that, but it's difficult to characterize the beginning of our acquaintance without some explanation.

We met, shortly after my previous boyfriend had inexplicably discarded me, on a dating website called planetout.com—this was in the four seconds during which there existed gay dating websites where you could arrange a date you weren't certain was going to end with your clothing on the floor, though I belonged to the other kind of website too, since sometimes when you're in the mood for your clothing to end up on the floor you don't want to risk having to keep it on—and I responded to Mike's initial message even though he used the word "impending" when he meant "incipient." I'm not sure whether it was my charmingly self-conscious neediness or the fact that I was a composer of musical theater that attracted him, but in either case he was good-looking enough that I was happy to write him back.

A month earlier, after a dinner so interminable it broke the laws of physics, I had started scheduling dates in the afternoon, so Mike and I met for the first time during lunch in midtown Manhattan at Café Edison, known to many in the theater community as the Polish Tea Room (since nobody in the theater community can afford to go to the Russian Tea Room) and spent an awkward hour together, by the end of which I knew that he wasn't my soul mate—he was too boring—but not whether he was entirely without merit, so we arranged to have dinner a few days later. During the after-dinner sex, he said, "Do you think we're going too fast?" and the look I gave him was filled with such contempt for the idea that it gave the rest of the encounter an aggressive character I found highly satisfying.

We began seeing each other with some frequency, though there was a little confusion as to what this signified. As far as I was concerned we were having casual sex and not-dating (note the hyphen), but when Mike referred to me one day as his boyfriend, I felt, though he could not have been more mistaken, that correcting him would almost certainly involve an uncomfortable conversation, and it seemed foolish to converse uncomfortably when I could be having sex instead. When I mentioned the incident on my anonymous blog, *The Search for Love in Manhattan*, several commenters cautioned me to take care, but what did they know anyway?

So I continued having casual sex with and not-dating Mike and blogging about it, and having casual sex with and not-dating several other men and blogging about it, and having casual sex unencumbered by not-dating with still more men and blogging about that, too. After nine months or so, Mike told me he was going to Boston for a year to get a degree in public health and I took the opportunity to dump him not that we were going out anyway because we weren't.

Mike is one of those weirdos, though, who stay friends with their exes, which he clearly thought I was even though I obviously wasn't. I don't really see the point of being friends with people who have had the bad judgment to stop sleeping with you, but saying no would have required more energy than saying yes, so there we were, friends for a year or so, until one night he said, "I was surfing the Web the other day and I read your blog."

Well, the long and the short of it, told in more detail in my hilarious and deeply moving book *Swish: My Quest to Become the Gayest Person Ever and What Ended Up Happening Instead*—which I wish I had called *Confessions of a Stereotype*, because the current title makes it seem like a piece of fluff, which it's not, so you should totally read it—is that I came clean, about everything: the extent to which I'd been having casual sex with and not-dating other men ("Oh, I figured that out," he said, "the day I saw bite marks on your ass"), the cavalier attitude I'd taken toward our relationship, my view of him as a *divertissement*. But the thing is, being honest felt so good that I started hanging out with him more, and eventually I asked him out, and he said yes—God knows why—and now, four years later, the opportunity to take it back had come and gone, so we were pretty much stuck with each other.

I appreciated this a great deal, because I couldn't imagine how anybody else would have stayed with me after what I'd put him through, which included a couple years of deep depression (mine, not his) during which he would try in vain to keep my attention as we conversed because I was either a) thinking about how he wasn't good enough for me, a train of thought I felt it my duty to share with him (he was in medical school and I was getting certified to be an aerobics instructor), or b) crying. *I* would have dumped me. "I'm a doctor," he said when I asked him later on how he had been able to stand it. "I know depression and anxiety aren't permanent."

Mind you, I'd put in my own time too, when during his residency he was on overnight call every other day, which meant that he cancelled on me nine times out of every ten we made plans, and the tenth time he was either so exhausted I might as well have been by myself or so irritated I wished I were, and I *still* made a delicious pie to bring to his parents' house on Thanksgiving, without consciously resenting it. I remember seeing a statistic before Mike graduated from med school that the divorce rate in psychiatric residencies was over 100 percent, which would mean that psychiatric residents got divorced, remarried, and got divorced again, and, while when I saw it I thought it was ridiculous, I'm now surprised the number isn't over 200 percent. (By the way: while Mike has no problem with anything I might write about him or our life together—a stance that baffles me utterly, but whatever, he's an alien from Mars—he's said he doesn't feel comfortable with my writing about his work, so let's just say that these days he runs an inpatient unit at a city psychiatric hospital and leave it at that.)

Then one day, when he had been in residency for a year, there was an article in the paper about a gay couple who had bought and renovated a dilapidated house through a program run by the Department of Housing and Urban Development, and before nightfall we had made a bid on a house in Crown Heights, the Brooklyn neighborhood famous for its drug dealers and for the race riot it had hosted in the nineties. The Department of Housing and Urban Development proved remarkably difficult to buy a house from, however, and then the economy went to hell, but eventually we moved in and managed to live together for a year and a half without producing a spectacular murder-suicide, at which point he knelt and proposed marriage to me.

The question of marriage had first entered our life as a couple in 2004, not long after we had started dating again, when the Massachusetts Supreme Court declared that preventing same-sex couples from marrying was unconstitutional (for a brief and highly biased legislative history of American marriage equality with respect to sexuality, see the appendix, "A Brief and Highly Biased Legislative History of American Marriage Equality With Respect to Sexuality"). In response, Jason West, the twenty-seven-year-old mayor of New Paltz, New York, not to be outdone by his neighbors to the north, announced that he would begin performing marriages of same-sex couples. He was stopped after several days by a restraining order and charged with nineteen misdemeanor counts of solemnizing marriages without a license, but New Paltz remained a metonym for marriage equality, and same-sexers kept going there and getting hitched; so many, in fact, that somebody in New Paltz started a waiting list to accommodate the hordes of same-sexers who wanted to take advantage of the city's legislative willingness to play fast and loose.

(In this book I'm sometimes going to use the term "same-sexer" rather than "gay." For better and for worse, "gay" as a descriptor of sexuality is an adjective often applied only to men, and men are not the only people interested in getting married. I find "LGBT" stylistically unacceptable as an adjective, though not quite as tragic as "lesbigay," which enjoyed a thankfully brief popularity in the early nineties; furthermore, use of such blanket terms to discuss marriage equality fails to take into account the fact that marriage laws can apply differently in different cases to bisexual and transgender people—the latter especially, given that in some states legal sex is what's on your driver's license and in others it's what's on your birth certificate. "Queer" has political connotations that lead many people to reject it as a label. Hence, "same-sexer": somebody who has relationships with or is attracted to people of the same legal sex. If it was good enough for Gore Vidal, it's good enough for me.)

My friends Rob and David signed up for the New Paltz waiting list, and when they got the call in June of 2004 I joined them, their dog Goblin, and Rob's friend Richard on a journey upstate. We arrived at the location, a tent outside a charming bed-and-breakfast, to find it filled with profusions of flowers and rainbow balloons. While Rob and David met with one of the people who would be performing ceremonies that day, I wandered around outside and looked at the other couples there to make their vows: four pairs of men and six pairs of women, one of which pairs I found so beautiful that I thought I would die if they told me I couldn't take a picture. Luckily they didn't, but I can't include the picture because, although the women look gorgeous in it, there's also this weird, slightly creepy guy behind them who ruins the effect. In any case, the day's weddings were going to be performed serially, in one morning-long event. Rob and David were somewhere in the middle of the schedule, so we settled back to watch the ceremonies before theirs.

The first couple to get married that day in New Paltz was a pair of short older men, dressed in suits. The ceremony was brief— three or four minutes—and they held hands the whole time. The celebrant was dressed in a white robe with a purple stole; her voice was low and pleasant, and the language she used was comfortingly traditional ("Do you promise to take this man," and so forth). At the end, she said, "I now pronounce you married," and I started to cry. The two men went back to their seats and another couple got up.

The weddings were being performed by alternating celebrants (evidently conducting illegal marriages takes a lot out of you) and the second, a low-and-pleasant-voiced man similarly dressed in a white robe with a purple stole, used similarly traditional language, and I was all set to cry again, when he said, "I now pronounce you *legally* married" (italics his, not mine), and I have no idea how I was able to keep myself from leaping out of my wooden folding chair, running up, wrapping my hands around his neck, and telling him if he didn't take it back and do it right I would choke the life out of him.

Because the couple he'd joined in holy matrimony (solve for some value of "holy") was *not* legally married. They had no marriage license, because the mayor had been enjoined from issuing one; in the absence of a license, their marriage was invalid in the eyes of the law—an unjust law, to be sure, and I think an unconstitutional one, but the law of the land nonetheless—and to claim otherwise, to *pretend* that what had just happened would be considered a legal marriage, was, as far as I was concerned, a gross insult to every one of us there and to every single person in this country and others working toward marriage equality.

Worst of all, the couple involved didn't even seem upset about the travesty being perpetrated upon them—they were just *standing* there, smiling, getting *married*, as if what they *really* cared about were declaring their *commitment* to each other in front of the assembled guests rather than flying into a towering rage because of a single word. Some people.

After a few moments, though, my fury began to abate, but I still spent the next three weddings terrified that Rob and David would get the I-now-pronounce-you-legally-married guy. Thankfully, they didn't, so their wedding was unmarred by the pretense that you could conquer injustice by calling it justice; furthermore, they took their dog Goblin up with them and stood holding her, which made the whole thing cuter than anybody could bear. I cried again, we sat through another four or five weddings—the couple in the picture did not have Mr. I-Now-Pronounce-You-Legally-Married, so I cried at their ceremony too (apparently my lacrimal glands turn into Stakhanovites at same-sex weddings, so if you're worried your friends won't get emotional enough at yours, give me a call)—and then drove back, giddy, to Manhattan.

When I told Mike about the event the next day, he asked, "Would you ever want to do something like that?," very carefully keeping the question in the abstract.

"No," I said. "I'm so happy for Rob and David, but for me it's legal marriage—unequivocally legal—or nothing."

"Why?"

I told him why.

If I had ever had any doubt that the government should be kept out of the business of language, it would have been eradicated utterly by the gallimaufry of terms assembled when the defenders of what has come to be known as "traditional marriage," knowing they couldn't deny same-sexers *some* sort of legal recognition for our relationships, made it nonetheless clear that actual marriage was off the table: domestic partnership, civil union, reciprocal beneficiaries, relationship of mutual interdependence.

"There's really a state that gives us relationships of mutual interdependence?" said Mike when I went through this list for him.

"Maryland."

"Well, they *are* below the Mason-Dixon Line."

People in these arrangements can typically do things like make funeral arrangements for each other and inherit each other's estates if one of them dies without a will, but not sue for child support or visitation rights or be excused from testifying against each other if called to the stand in state court. In some states they can add each other's names to the deed of a residence with no tax liability but only after swearing an affidavit and producing two documents proving they even have a relationship in the first place. (Lucky same-sexers in New York State, if their deceased domestic partner was a member of the City Council, also have the right, according to Ad. Code § 3-204.2, to buy the chair he or she sat in at Council meetings for fair market value.)

Even when the legal status in question offers, on paper, all the benefits of marriage, in real life it doesn't always end up working out like that. Your sister makes you and your domestic partner stay in separate rooms when you come to town for the family reunion because you're not married, for example, or you can't open a line of credit at the bank because the computer system has options for "single" and "married" but not for "in a relationship of mutual interdependence" (seriously, Maryland, that was the best you could do?).

And sometimes it's a lot worse, even if you've made every legal arrangement available to you. When Janice Langbehn and Lisa-Marie Pond were on vacation in Florida with their four adopted kids (of the twenty-six they'd fostered: "Lesbians," said Mike when I told him this story) and Pond had an aneurysm, hospital workers wouldn't allow Langbehn or the children in to see her because the two weren't married, and Pond spent the next eight hours dying alone. Louise Walpin and Marsha Shapiro were thrilled when New Jersey passed a civil-union law in 2006, because it meant they could get more health insurance to take care of their son Aaron, born with severe mental and physical disabilities, but company after company told Walpin they didn't offer health benefits for civilly united couples—even though they were legally obligated to do so—and the two went into hundreds of thousands of dollars' worth of debt to pay for Aaron's medical care before he died in 2008.

The example that shocks me the most, however, is that of Clay Greene and Harold Scull, who lived together in Sonoma County, California. Each had written a will making the other his beneficiary, each had granted the other power of attorney, each had named the other in his medical directives—if it was possible to sign a document, they'd signed it. Which was why, when Scull, eighty-eight, fell on the steps of their house and was taken to the hospital in 2009, Greene, seventy-seven, expected to be consulted from the beginning, as was required by law. Instead, however, he was forbidden to see Scull at the hospital. Then county health care workers put Scull in a nursing home and refused to tell Greene where it was or even what it was called. Then, without even letting Greene go back home to collect any of his belongings or his mementos of Scull, they put him in a nursing home too—a different one, and against his will—and went to court, explaining that they needed to make financial decisions on Scull's behalf because his "roommate" shouldn't be the one to do it. They sold the contents of the house the two leased together (in order to pay for Scull's medical care), except for the few knickknacks workers pocketed to take home ("This would look nice in my living room," said one; another, "My wife will love this"), terminated their lease, gave their apartment back to the landlord, and *abandoned their cat at the pound.* Scull died three months later, Greene still begging for the name of his nursing home. Greene was finally released from his own nursing home and filed suit against Sonoma County, which recently settled for $600,000.

"That number," said Mike when he heard about the case, "is missing a few zeroes."

The fact that people often don't know about or simply disregard these McMarriage laws isn't the only thing wrong with them. Another glaring problem is that they function only on the state level, leaving questions of federal marriage law untouched. In 2004, the U.S. General Accounting Office reviewed the United States law codes and counted 1,138 federal benefits to which married couples are entitled. President Obama has told America he supports same-sexers' right to marry, and the Defense of Marriage Act signed into treacherous law by President Clinton seems to be headed for the dustbin, but it's still a far cry from where we are now to full marriage equality. (Of course, by the time you read this, the Supreme Court may very well have ruled in *Hollingsworth v. Perry* and *U.S. v. Windsor,* and if their excellent opinion from 2003 in *Lawrence v. Texas* striking down Texas's risible sodomy statute is any indication, they might even have made the right decision, in which case I don't know, maybe you should just stop reading and go out for some ice cream or something.) In any case, here are some highlights of the things that would not have been available to me as Mike's domestic partner and that in fact are not available to me in February of 2013 even though (spoiler alert) Mike and I are married.

If Mike dies, I don't get his Social Security benefits. (He doesn't get mine if I die, either, but my employment history is such that my benefits are likely to be all but worthless.)

If one of us becomes aged, blind, or disabled, the other can't get Supplemental Security Income assistance to take care of him.

We're considered inessential when it comes to each other's Medicaid benefits.

If we lose everything to Nigerian Internet scammers or another banking collapse, we'll be ineligible for federal support for low-income family housing.

If I go to war, Mike won't be compensated if I disappear, won't get any additional disability compensation if I'm disabled, won't get my pension if I die, won't get military life insurance, won't get government medical care, won't get any educational assistance or job training, and, if I'm buried in a military cemetery, can't be buried with me. (I choose myself rather than Mike to go to war because I have a lot of fantasies about killing people who make me angry, though to be honest those fantasies involve a lot of torture beforehand that probably isn't sanctioned by the Geneva Conventions.)

If it turns out that he was actually born in another country and his visa runs out or he's here illegally, he'll be deported no matter how long we've been together, though with luck the Uniting American Families Act pending in Congress (at least as of early 2013) will rectify this situation.

The list goes on and on.

(I actually think that marriage shouldn't be a prerequisite for access to most, if not all, of these benefits in the first place. There are same-sexers who agree with me who argue that it's the institution of marriage that is the problem; I understand where they're coming from, but I think universal health care and housing will be a lot easier to accomplish than the abolition of marriage itself.)

Some of the rights I've mentioned can be gained by drawing up legal arrangements, but only in exchange for thousands if not tens of thousands of dollars in legal fees, and not necessarily to any effect—the documents Janice Langbehn, Lisa-Marie Pond, Louise Walpin, Marsha Shapiro, Harold Scull, and Clay Greene had signed didn't help them much when push came to shove.

On the other hand, if I open a flower shop, Mike's salary won't be counted in determining whether I meet the income cap for assistance under the Fresh Cut Flowers and Fresh Cut Greens Promotion and Information Act of 1993, so in the end I guess it all balances out.

The thing is, though, being denied the rights currently available to married straight people isn't really my problem. I'm not interested in interacting with a child until it's old enough to discuss Kafka, so questions of child support are moot, and I don't need Medicaid benefits yet (though ask me again in forty years and we'll see what my answer is then). Right now, I don't experience the lack of access to most of those 1,138 privileges as particularly onerous. What I do experience as particularly onerous is this:

I'm a grown man chained to the kids' table.

Marriage is a public, legally approved way to declare that you're willing to be charged with the well-being of another human. The whole for-richer-or-for-poorer-in-sickness-and-in-health thing isn't there to make sure you have an easier time dealing with the embassy when you're in Cabo. It's not there to give you tax breaks (which would be useless to us anyway, as my finances are irregular enough that any time I suggest merging our assets and accounts Mike sticks his fingers in his ears and goes, "La la la la la," and besides, I avoid taking loopholes because I think it's unpatriotic to try to pay less in taxes than you owe). No; marriage is there so you can tell your boyfriend that if something bad happens to him you'll support him—and so other people can see you tell him that. Marriage lets you accept a responsibility in such a way that society can hold you to it.

The purpose of government, according to Thomas Jefferson, is "to enable the people of a nation to live in safety and happiness." So if the representatives of my government forbid me to marry, I have to assume they believe it would threaten the safety and happiness of the American people to allow me to be responsible for someone I love. And what other reason can there be for this than that they think I'm too weak to bear that responsibility?

I am, in the eyes of the law, a creature incapable of full human development.

How, at base, is this any different than being told, by men and women I grew up with, no less, that there is not a seat for me with them at the grown-ups' table and there never will be so I should just get used to the plastic utensils and enjoy the finger paint?

There are people who are like, oh, marriage equality is a good thing because it will force same-sexers to grow up and start acting like heterosexual married couples. Jonathan Rauch, in his terrific book *Marriage: Why It Is Good for Gays, Good for Straights, and Good for America*, writes that gay culture, "with its elevation of play over work and of self-expression over discipline and of youth over everything . . . seem[s] to suffer from an advanced case of Peter Pan syndrome." (He's talking about gay male culture; if female same-sexers have a common problem, it's not a refusal to grow up. "Overprocessing," offered one lesbian I asked; "Birkenstocks," another. "If the women I've been dating are any indication," said a third, "cat allergies.")

On one hand, it's difficult for me not to feel that Rauch and others who take this position have something of the Uncle Tom in them, as if they were saying, look how selfish and immature we gay men are, but if you let us get married we'll be able to become better people like you. At the same time, however, I can't say that I'm against giving gay men the *opportunity* to grow up if we want to.

Which is why I feel so ambivalent about the "marriage will force gay men to mature" argument. Yes, the legal right to marry will allow us to assume adulthood in a way that has been forbidden us for centuries, if not millennia. On the other hand, forcing us to

be children and then blaming us for acting selfish and immature—
you might as well burn down a house to prove it was made of ash.

Let's say that the Defenders of Traditional Marriage are right and
that the institution of marriage is in terrible danger.

The problem is, it's not the kind of danger they're talking
about.

And they're the ones creating it.

The current attack on marriage, if such an attack exists, began,
as far as I'm concerned, on October 11, 1991, when Berkeley, California, became the first city in the United States to register legal
relationships that offered access to some but not all of the rights
and responsibilities of marriage. On that day, twenty-nine couples
went to City Hall and, before city employees, officially declared
their commitment to each other by becoming domestic partners,
and the erosion of marriage began. Because twenty-eight of those
couples were same-sex.

But one was straight.

On October 11, 1991, my first year of college, two people who
could have gotten married more easily than they could have
spelled each other's names gained official recognition for their
partnership without the benefit of marriage.

And marriage, if you're inclined to such a way of thinking, has
been in danger ever since.

A look at a possible future: In 1999, the French government
created the *pacte civil de solidarité* (civil solidarity pact), a marriage-
lite status like the ones in many American states that allow couples
most of the privileges of marriage without the name. That year,
6,000 couples chose to unite in a civil solidarity pact—and of
those couples, 2,520 were straight. In 2010, there were 205,558 civil
solidarity pacts, *196,415 of which* were between heterosexuals.
There is now one civil solidarity pact for every two weddings
performed in France, and *94 percent of those pacts are made by
straight couples.* As of 2010, of the approximately 900,000 civil

solidarity pacts made in the decade since the creation of the status, some 835,000 were between straight people who could have gotten married but chose instead to do something different. Since the creation of the civil solidarity pact, the number of heterosexual marriages performed in France, which had been holding steady up till that point, has fallen by an average of 5,000 per year. That's over 500,000 potential heterosexual marriages in France destroyed — not by marriages of same-sex couples but by the attempts of the Defenders of Traditional Marriage to prevent such marriages. (In early 2013, France finally repented of its squeamishness and now same-sexers can wed, but given the civil solidarity pact statistics one fears it may already be too late for the institution of French marriage.)

I assume that French enthusiasm for the civil solidarity pact is at least in part a reaction against the country's heavily Catholic history, but America, without that history, is beginning to have some statistics of its own, and if you're of the marriage-is-in-danger school you won't find them reassuring. Between June 1 of 2011 and May 31 of 2012, the first year civil-union licenses were available in Cook County, Illinois, for example, 212 of the 2,504 issued were for straight couples. How many tens or hundreds of thousands of potential heterosexual American marriages will Illinois's civil union law destroy in the next ten years?

In *Marriage: Love and Life in the Divine Plan*, a pastoral letter issued in 2009 by the United States Conference of Catholic Bishops, the ecclesiasts of the largest religion in the world tell us they are "troubled that far too many people do not understand what it means to say that marriage . . . is a blessing and a gift from God. . . . Young people esteem marriage as an ideal but can be reluctant to make the actual commitment necessary to enter and sustain it. Some choose instead to live in cohabiting relationships that may or may not lead to marriage and can be detrimental to the well-being of their children and themselves."

Can the members of the United States Conference of Catholic Bishops be pleased that, as more and more states create alternatives to marriage, trying desperately to keep same-sex couples from full equality, young people reluctant to make the commitment have more and more legally sanctioned options to forgo the hassle of the vows and the solemnity and the till-death-do-us-part and skip right to the tax benefits?

It's been a while since I slept with a Catholic bishop, but I have to believe the answer is no.

Notice, by the way, that with the exception of the subtitle of this book I am avoiding the phrase "gay marriage." This is because I think, along with Evan Wolfson, founder of the marriage-equality organization Freedom to Marry and author of *Why Marriage Matters: America, Equality, and Gay People's Right to Marry,* that the sooner we're rid of it, the better. As I see it, any adjectival qualification can only limit the idea of marriage, can only make it less than just plain marriage. In 1967, Richard and Mildred Loving, the couple who took Virginia's anti-miscegenation statute to the Supreme Court and watched it topple into oblivion, didn't want to get interracial married; they wanted to get married. In ancient Rome, low-ranking soldiers were for a time forbidden to marry; those who found this burdensome didn't want, one presumes, to get military married; they wanted to get married.

I didn't want to get gay married.

I wanted to get *married.*

(Of course, comedienne Liz Feldman said all this much more succinctly: "It's very dear to me, the issue of gay marriage. Or, as I like to call it, 'marriage.' You know, because I had lunch this afternoon, not gay lunch. I parked my car, I didn't gay park it.")

The practical result for me of all these arguments about marriage was that, since I was unwilling to accept any store-brand knock-offs, Mike's proposal in 2007 was in a way completely theoretical:

there was nowhere in the United States he and I could wed. (Same-sexers could marry in Massachusetts, true, but, except in rare cases, only if they lived there.)

And then the California Supreme Court ruled that the law banning marriage equality in that state was unconstitutional. And since California had no problem granting marriage licenses to out-of-staters, this meant that Mike and I could now marry each other legally in the United States.

When I read about the decision, on May 15, 2008, at 3:30 in the afternoon (it had been issued at 2:00 but I had a deadline for an article at 3:00 and then I had to spend half an hour looking at pictures of naked men online), I burst into uncontrollable sobs, because I had just been released from a cage I hadn't known I was in.

I have a tendency, my friends have been unkind enough to note on occasion, to hyperbole. But in this case I mean exactly what I say; I really couldn't control the sobs. I sobbed and wept and wailed for an hour and a half, and every time I tried to stop I just got louder. I started worrying that I was alarming my neighbors, and since my neighbors were crack dealers (on the right) and a really judgmental schoolteacher (on the left, and much more frightening) I didn't see how bothering them would do me any good.

Finally I thought, *All right, this is getting ridiculous. If I don't do something soon I'll dehydrate myself. . . . I know, I'll go shopping!* I tried to work up the motivation to walk to the Key Foods three blocks away, but it always seems so far and I'd already exhausted most of my energy in bawling, so I went to the more expensive Met Foods around the corner.

And the thing is: *shopping felt different.*

As I picked up a pint of chocolate peanut butter truffle ice cream, I thought, *I am buying this ice cream as somebody with the right to be married.*

As I put the grasshopper cookies into my cart, I thought, *I am buying these cookies as somebody who very well may, at some point in the foreseeable future, be married.*

As I dropped the pound of M&Ms onto the conveyor at the checkout, I thought, *On the other hand maybe I should put these back, or I might not end up getting married after all.*

I don't know how to explain it. I was no different than I'd been at noon. Federal law was no different. New York State law was no different. But I was living in a world that felt like it had just become a little fairer.

Naturally, Mike and I started making plans to go out to California to stay with my relatives and get legally married there—we'd do the actual ceremony with guests and flowers and stuff back east, since all my friends were writers and actors and therefore too poor to travel to the west coast for an event at which I could guarantee them neither the possibility of publication/production nor sex—and, naturally, I immediately ruined those plans, by going to Los Angeles to give a reading for *Swish* and not telling my aunt Suzie I was there.

Suzie has been my surrogate mother for twenty years, ever since my biological mother died; an actual fairy godmother could not have supported me more devotedly. My only excuse for not calling her was that I found the whole trip overwhelming and I really wanted nothing more than just to stay in my hotel room watching TV and eating candy from the mini-bar. Karma charged me dearly for my neglect; the reading, in a cavernous room, was attended by a humiliating five people, which pulled me right back to my senior year of high school, when I invited the whole class to my birthday party and three people came. This time around I tried for like forty-five seconds to give a reading and then gave up and sat down and had a conversation with the people who had shown up, which ended up being a slightly mind-blowing exploration of same-sexer history, since the oldest person there was seventy and the youngest was twenty. When the seventy-year-old said he still couldn't fathom the idea that gay people could get married, the twenty-year-old said, "Oh, God, all it means to me is that my mother has started calling me all the time, asking me when my boyfriend and I are going to tie the knot already, and it's driving me crazy."

But I hadn't paid enough in shame; a few weeks later one of my cousins learned that I'd been there and enough of the Los Angeles branch of my family got (rightly) upset enough that going out to Los Angeles to stay with them and get married became a tricky proposition. Mike and I decided therefore to delay.

This delay turned out to be costly, but it might very well have been for the best. "We construct marriage and its meaning," writes Julia Sullivan in *Conversations With My Friends*, "out of the examples that our families put before us." And if that was true, then Mike and I had some pretty complex building materials to figure out.

2

Researching
Family Marriage Traditions

In the meantime, while I figured out a way to apologize to my family in Los Angeles, I figured I ought to get Mike an engagement ring, if only so that if he went to a bar he would now be forced to expend a modicum of effort to appear available, though since his bar visits coincide with the appearances of Halley's Comet I didn't have much to worry about. The problem was that the ring Mike had given me was Cartier, and the oceans of money that publishing a book and writing musicals had brought me left me just shy of a position to buy him a ring made by Mattel. I was absolutely certain I could afford one of those lollipop rings, but at the age of thirty-seven I felt I ought to aim higher. Eventually I hit upon a brilliant idea, which was to give Mike the ring my father had worn while married to my mother. My father assented to this plan and said he'd send me the ring as soon as he could find it.

The thing is, the plan to use my dad's wedding ring was not unproblematic. My parents had an unusual courtship, and I wasn't sure that adding its echo to our ceremony was the right idea.

In 1967, my father, who was married to a woman named Marcy, worked at the Washington, D.C., law firm of Covington & Burling, where he had the worst secretary in the world. I have tried and tried to get him to tell me what made her so awful, but evidently she so traumatized him that he's repressed all specific memories of her; in any case, one day she told him she'd been offered a job with one of Covington & Burling's clients, a railroad company, and that the job was so good it would be hard for her to turn down. "Amy, as much as it pains me," said my father with a straight face, "I *cannot* stand in your way." Then he went home and threw a party.

The next day he went to the head of the steno pool and said, "Barbara, I need a new secretary, and I'd like Mrs. Ward." Mary Frances Ward had worked for him a few times, when Amy was out sick or when he needed additional help with a project, and he had found her both skilled and amiable.

"That's too bad," said Barbara, "because you can't have her."

"Why not?" he asked.

"She doesn't know shorthand. And we don't assign secretaries who don't know shorthand to individual lawyers. They have to stay in the steno pool."

"Well, then, that's perfect," said my father, "because I don't do dictation."

"You still can't have her," said Barbara.

"Why not?"

"She's too valuable in the pool. I'm not willing to give her up."

"Well, I want her."

"That's nice. You can't have her."

A day or two later my father passed Mrs. Ward in the hall and she took the opportunity to tell him how much she appreciated his request. "But they won't let me. I don't know shorthand."

"Well, we'll see, won't we?" said my father with what I like to imagine was an impish grin. And a few days later Mrs. Ward was assigned to be his secretary.

"She was terrific," he said, sipping Coke in my kitchen when I finally got him to tell me this story a few years ago. "She typed 100 words a minute, in those old days, before computers, was brilliant, knew everything—in fact, for the first time, and probably almost the last time, I was able to tell a secretary, 'Write him a letter saying such-and-so,' and then I'd get back a letter saying it better than I could have written it myself."

Mrs. Ward was not without her own inner imp. When my father's typewriter stopped working, for example, she came over to his desk, took a look at it, and said, "Oh, you just need to replace the fan belt."

"A typewriter has a fan belt?" my father asked.

"Sure. It's just like a car," she assured him. "The moving parts break down." So my father called the office manager and asked for a replacement fan belt.

"Typewriters don't have fan belts," said the office manager. "Your secretary must be Mrs. Ward."

Employees of Covington & Burling worked a half-day every weekend, so when one Saturday my father finished early he asked Mrs. Ward whether she wanted to get a sandwich for lunch with him. I must be very, very clear that this was not a date. Not only were they both married, my father was at the time even more socially imperceptive than he is now, and two years ago the rent boy was actually taking his clothes off in my father's hotel room before he realized what was happening.

"Sure," said Mrs. Ward. "I'll just call my husband when we're done." (She didn't drive, which meant that her husband, Freddy, brought her to work and picked her up at the end of the day.) So she and my father took a walk and sat outside in the park, eating sandwiches and talking about things that had nothing to do with work. Three hours later, they got back to the office and she called Freddy to come pick her up.

On Monday, when my dad came in, her first words to him were, "I'm sorry, Mr. Derfner, but I can't work for you anymore."

"What?" my father said.

"My husband was really mad on Saturday that I took so long at lunch and came home so late, and he says I can't work for you anymore."

"What?" repeated my father. "I don't get it. Let's get some sandwiches at lunch and talk about this." And when lunchtime came they walked down to the grassy area behind the White House, where the story came out.

"Freddy called a bunch of times to pick me up on Saturday afternoon," she said, "and the girl who answered the phone said, 'She went out to have a sandwich with her boss.' The first couple of times that wasn't a problem, but he kept calling and he kept getting the same answer, and when he finally came to pick me up, he said, 'Okay, there's still time.' And I said to him, 'Time for what?' He said, 'Time to go to confession.' I said, 'Wha—? Freddy, nothing happened. We didn't—we had lunch, we had sandwiches, we talked.'"

So Mrs. Ward and my father continued trying to figure out what to do about the situation, and at some point she said, "The problem is, I could be veering in that direction."

"And that," my father told me, "hit me like a punch in the side of the head. And I said the immortal, classic, Shakespearean words: 'You'd be pretty easy to veer toward too.'"

Iacta alea est.

"Well, look," said my father finally, "I still want you to work for me."

"I still want to work for you."

"Maybe you can talk some sense into him? Change his mind?"

"Well," she said, "I'll try, but I'm not sure it'll do any good." And indeed, when she came in the next morning, it was to report that her efforts had yielded no fruit; Freddy was still insistent that she have nothing more to do with her boss.

"Okay," said my dad. "Uh . . . let's get a sandwich and talk about it again."

"When I got married the first time," he explained to me, "Marcy and I were just kids, you know, and sort of inexperienced—not so much inexperienced at anything in particular, but just inexperienced in life. The marriage was okay while we were at Yale, while I was in law school, which was the first two years. It was a hothouse, and we could flourish. After we moved to

Washington, it just didn't work, for a whole bunch of reasons. You grow, you become different people, whatever it was. And the way I measured it was in terms of my disposition. I like to think that I'm basically not a grouchy guy, I'm a sunny guy. But I had just become a grouch. For example, two years in a row at Covington & Burling I was voted Sunshine Man of the Year. I was so dumb I thought it was a compliment. But that day in the park I just felt so light, so good."

They began an affair.

She told Freddy about it almost immediately, and within the week he had moved out, so my father spent a lot of time at her apartment, doing what people having affairs usually do and listening to music in between. "The song we played most often," my father told me, "was Glen Campbell's 'Gentle on My Mind.' It talks about leaving somebody, and leaving her crying, but we were so happy."

Then, one weekend, my father's wife went to Pennsylvania to visit her parents, and he spent the entire weekend with Mrs. Ward, agonizing. "I knew what my mind and my heart were telling me," he said to me, "but it was an alien process. When I was growing up, we had this one distant cousin, we called him 'Stanley, the divorced one.' I'm serious. I never heard of anybody who got divorced. When I was in Washington I'd heard of a few more, but it was still something very strange." By the end of the weekend he had yet to come to a decision.

Fast forward to Monday morning. ("You can't do that!" I screamed at him in my kitchen. "Do you want to hear the story or don't you?" he said, and I shut my mouth.) My dad came in to work and on his desk was Glen Campbell's album *Gentle on My Mind*. And Mrs. Ward had left him a note that said, "I know you couldn't leave Marcy. I will treasure forever the moments we've had. I don't blame you for anything, because it's been wonderful for me. And this record is just a symbol of my love."

So he went into the secretaries' office and asked the other secretaries to give him and Mrs. Ward a few minutes. "Mary

Frances," he said, "I left Marcy last night." And the rest of the moment was, he vows, like a Hollywood movie.

By this time, he had already gotten a call from the Lawyers Constitutional Defense Committee about whether he would move to Mississippi to do civil rights work; after mulling it over for a while, he decided he would go. When the news transpired, Mrs. Ward was called into the office of Mr. Burling, one of the firm's founding partners. "Mrs. Ward," he said, looking stern, "I understand that you and Armand are thinking of leaving." And she said nervously, yes, that's right, but I've had a wonderful time working here, it's been such a rewarding experience. "Armand Derfner is a *brilliant* young lawyer," he said, "with a *bright future* here." Burling was apparently an imposing man, and the longer he looked at her the more frightened she grew. "But," he said finally, "there are a lot of brilliant young lawyers with bright futures here, so losing him won't be a problem. Would *you* be willing to stay?"

"And that was the beginning," my father told me, "of twenty-five beautiful years. Some hard years, no question about it. But she had been told as a teenager, when she was diagnosed with diabetes, 'You're not going to live very long, don't bother getting married, finishing school, you won't have children, anything like that.' So I always thought that whatever I had with Mom was a gift that she wasn't expecting to have."

"So what you're saying," said Mike when I told him this story, "is that your parents were homewreckers."

"Well, homewreckers whose work together made it possible to practice civil rights law in this country," I said—my mother wrote the law that allows lawyers who win civil rights cases to be paid by the corporations and government agencies that lose rather than by their clients, who rarely have two chickens to rub together—"but yeah, homewreckers nonetheless."

I once asked my dad's sister what Marcy had been like. She looked at me blankly and said, "Marcy?"

"Dad's first wife," I said.

"Oh, you mean the poisonous bitch," she said.

"I guess you've answered my question."

"I don't mean that in a bad way."

The only thing I remember my mom ever saying about Freddy was that she should have known they were doomed when he came back from a trip out of town and was furious to find that she'd written a check for $100 (worth about $650 today) to a charity her grandmother supported. "I could have used that money," he said, "to buy a pair of shoes." Then again, when she died in 1992 he did come to her memorial service, which I thought was pretty classy.

A couple weeks after Mike and I came up with our plan for the other engagement ring I realized I might be in trouble, because Dad called to tell me he couldn't find the ring he wore when he was married to my mom. "I'll call Gigi," he said, referring to my mom's half-sister. "She may know where it is, or at least know where Mom's dad's ring might be."

But using my maternal grandfather's wedding ring would be symbolically much worse, given that he was only one of what turned out to be nine men my grandmother married (seven if you don't count the annulment and the common-law bigamy, but in for a penny, in for a pound, I say).

My mother's mother, who had spent four years in Paris and whom we therefore called, at her request, "Mémé," was short and reeked of perfume, which I loved. The other sense memory she conjures up is the clinking of her rings, which seemed to me to number in the thousands. She was able so to bejewel herself because her grandfather had been some sort of New York real estate mogul, which meant that the family owned things like the Waldorf

Astoria, the Omni Berkshire, and the ABC building. (This never helped me much; they sold everything for pennies in the early 1970s when the city went broke, because New York was a town whose time had obviously come and gone, and then spent it all. On rings, apparently.)

Mémé's paternal ancestry, however, while it made her rich, also made her Jewish, if not in the eyes of Jews then at least in the eyes of certain circles of society to which she was never able to gain full admittance. At my mother's funeral, when I was twenty, my father's mother, who went by the much homelier moniker "Grandma," went up to Mémé to offer her condolences on the death of her daughter. "A parent should never outlive a child," said Grandma in her thick Yiddish accent.

"What Armand needs to do now," said Mémé after thanking her, "is find a nice Jewish girl to marry."

"He did. He was married to her for twenty-five years."

"Mary Frances was *not Jewish!*" Mémé hissed. "She was a good Christian! She read her Bible every day!" (We didn't have a Bible in the house.) "My daughter was *not Jewish!*"

Grandma looked Mémé in the eye calmly and said, "She was Jewish enough for us."

As a child I found Mémé an incredibly compelling figure, and it's not difficult to think of her now as a sort of evil Auntie Mame. When I was eight she begged and begged my parents to let her take me to Afghanistan so I could see the Khyber Pass by moonlight (this was in the eighties, when during the Soviet invasion Afghanistan was littered with land mines that ultimately killed a million Afghan civilians). At the same time, whenever I came back from her house, holding, like Persephone returning from Hades, a pomegranate from her pomegranate tree, I would subject my civil-rights-worker parents to a righteous monologue about something like the travesty of justice that was the graduated income tax. When I was a baby, apparently, on a visit to our house Mémé said something about how the niggers were ruining everything, to which my normally conflict-avoidant mother responded, "Mother, the next time this child hears you say that word will be the last time you see him until the day you die." I have no memory of hearing the word issue from Mémé's mouth, so she must have paid attention.

Here's what I know about Mémé's husbands (numbering from 1–9).

Her marriage with husband #1 she annulled after four days because he'd said he had money and he didn't.

With husband #2 she produced my Uncle Bill, who to this day on the rare occasions when he calls his father and says, hi, Dad, it's your son, Bill, receives the answer, I don't have a son.

Husband #3 was my mom's father, an engineer for the Navy.

Husband #4 was actually married to somebody else, or maybe it was Mémé who was married to somebody else, but they lived together for long enough that if nobody had been married to anybody else it would have been a common-law marriage, so I think of their relationship as common-law bigamy. He was a lawyer and my mom's (and her siblings') favorite of all her stepfathers, until she came home from school one day to find him hanging by the neck from a rafter with the stool kicked out from under him.

Husband #5 was some sort of tennis champion.

Husband #6 was both a member of the House Un-American Activities Committee and a Quaker, which I always thought was unbeatable, but then along came Paul Ryan with Ayn Rand and Jesus, so there you go.

Husband #7—the first one I was alive to meet—was a Frenchman with an Italian title (I remember it as Conte di Lumazon, but I can't find any evidence of such a title ever having existed) who wanted my mother to renounce her father so that she could be a viscountess and eventually inherit his rank. I am still furious that she refused, because if she hadn't I could have found a way to interpret the rules of heritability, Italian nobility being infamously flexible, so that upon her death I would have become a count and people would have to address me as "My Lord." The count was also, if memory serves, a French royalist and an arms smuggler, which fact became clear when my babysitting aunt called my mother and asked whether she ought to do anything about all the guns he and his friends had piled up on the piano.

Marriage #8 was to a truly wretched Englishman named Archie. He would do things like insist, on the way to Christmas morning at my great-grandmother's house, that we stop to get batteries in case we needed them for any gifts, and then, when we walked in late, say he was sorry but my dad just *had* to stop and get batteries. Once, when Hannukah and Christmas overlapped, we were having a quiet little Hannukah celebration in one part of the house, and Archie began blaring Christmas carols at full volume from the stereo ("I still don't understand why I stopped your uncle Bill from strangling him to death," my dad says). The *pièce de résistance*, though, was definitely when Mémé decided to take in a woman and her son who had been staying at the local women's shelter. As soon as she told him what she was planning to do, Archie installed locks on all the cabinets and the refrigerator so that, if their guests got hungry, they wouldn't be able to do anything about it, and then, the first day they were there, when the son left his breakfast bowl of Rice Krispies unfinished, Archie made him *fish the leftovers out of the garbage can and eat them*. No one was surprised when, after Archie's death, we found all sorts of malevolent-magic paraphernalia in his closet (an inscribed dagger, a cauldron, you name it)—and I'm all for Wiccans but I guarantee you that if he ever used these things it was to injurious purpose.

(My father was with Mémé when she filled out the marriage license application before her wedding to Archie. He says that, after checking the box indicating she'd been married before, she answered the question "How many husbands have you had [1, 2, etc.]?" by writing "3." "What?" she said when he looked at her agog. "It's obviously what comes next.")

Marriage #9 was to a former doctor about whom I remember only that a) he'd had his medical license revoked for incompetence, b) an avid gardener, he set the kitchen on fire when at one point he used the microwave to sterilize some potting soil, and c) once, after spending several minutes examining my mother's plastic ficus tree, he said to her, "You know, with a new pot and some watering, this plant could really thrive."

One day I told an elderly friend about my much-married grandmother and her face lit up. "What an optimist!" she exclaimed.

"What?" I said.

"She never stopped trying!"

Which, while true from a certain vantage point, wasn't particularly how I wanted to solemnize my marriage to Mike.

Because even if my aunt came up with a wedding ring from my grandmother's jewelry stash, how could I be sure I wasn't consecrating Mike to me with a ring worn by a member of HUAC or a French royalist arms smuggler?

"That," said Mike when I told him about Mémé, "explains so much about you."

"In a good way, I hope," I said.

"That explains so much about you."

When I called Dad again to ask about the search, he said he hadn't gotten any further in finding the ring. He was waiting for Gigi (I can never remember which husband she came from) to call him back, he said, but now Mike was very nervous, because a third possibility, frightening if unlikely, had occurred to me: what if I ended up giving him the wedding ring that marked the union of my great-great-grandparents the poisoners?

In the summer of 1910, my mother's father's father's father, forty-year-old insurance superintendent Frederick Henry Seddon, his wife, Margaret, their five children (two sons and three daughters), his father, and their servant moved into a large house in Leeds,

England. It was a neighborhood on the upswing; the Seddons were going places.

Before long, there was another addition to the household in Miss Eliza "Chickie" Barrow. Also in her forties, and exceedingly wealthy, Miss Barrow arrived at 63 Tollington Park after having lived with a succession of relatives and friends, all of whom had taken her in for her money but had eventually kicked her out both because she was querulous and slovenly and alcoholic and her relatives never knew whether she was going to be nice to them or yell at them and spit in their faces, and because she was virtually deaf and the only way they could communicate anything to her was to tell it to the small orphan she kept about her so he could shout things in her ear and whom she controlled by shaking him, shouting at him, and threatening to throw herself out the window if he didn't behave. Her hosts stood her and the small orphan as long as they could, because it really was a good deal of money, but eventually further hospitality was made impossible by the fact that, in addition to the idiosyncrasies I have detailed, she also suffered continually from bouts of particularly noxious diarrhea.

The Seddons, however, when her despairing cousins responded to their room-to-let ad and moved her in, simply put her on her own floor of their house, where the diarrhea didn't cause anybody else problems, except, one assumes, the laundress. The small orphan was unfazed by it, having developed, fortuitously, an adenoidal condition that robbed him of his sense of smell.

The household ran quite smoothly for a while, despite the challenges presented by Miss Barrow and by the Seddons' servant, Mary, who spent most of her time telling people about how her enemies were out to get her, except on those occasions when she broke into violent fits of screaming at people who weren't there. Margaret ran a dress shop, Frederick either seduced or raped women in the houses he insured (I can't figure out how to interpret the quote, "it is said of him that, with regard to women, he abused his position as an insurance superintendent with constant access to houses during the absence of the husband"), and everybody was happy, more or less. Meanwhile, the Seddons managed to persuade Chickie to transfer more and more of her money to them, starting with £1,600 worth of India stock (about $169,000 in today's American money) and continuing with some sort of lease on a pub worth £1,300 ($137,000) that brought in £120 a year ($12,500), until they owned about £3,000 ($316,500) worth of her property, in exchange for an annuity of £1 a week ($105 today) for the rest of her life; this left about £1,000 ($105,500) in her possession, some in banknotes, some in the bank, and some in gold coin in the lockbox in her room.

The Seddons did nothing by halves, however, so after Chickie had lived with them for a while, Margaret cashed the banknotes one by one under a false name and then, in June of 1911, took her tenant to the bank, where Chickie withdrew the £216 ($23,000) she had deposited there—giving it to Margaret to take care of, naturally—at which point there was only the £676 ($71,500) in gold coins in the lockbox. A few weeks later Margaret went to the pharmacy and bought a package of flypaper under a false name; she and her husband soaked the flypaper in water to leach out the arsenic, poured the arsenic-filled water into a bottle of a tonic Miss Barrow took regularly named, thrillingly, Valentine's Meat Juice, and the rest took care of itself. Since the symptoms of arsenic poisoning include terrible diarrhea, when the already valetudinarian Miss Barrow responded poorly to the new addition to her daily regimen, nothing seemed unusual.

Chickie Barrow died in short order, fallen victim to, as the doctor who signed her death certificate put it, "epidemic diarrhœa." That night Margaret went out to the music hall; the next day, after sending Chickie's cousins a letter to an address where he knew they no longer lived, Seddon took her diamond ring and gold watch to the jeweler, the ring to be resized for him, the gold watch to be stripped of its inscription to "E.J. Barrow, 1860" and reinscribed to his wife. The undertaker told him that a proper funeral would cost £4 ($422); Seddon said that he'd only found

£4 10s ($475) in her room, a sum that wouldn't cover the combined expenses of such a funeral and the doctor's bill, so the undertaker dropped his price and buried her in an unmarked public grave, paying Seddon a commission, of course, for the referral.

Apparently the small orphan failed to show up at school for a few days in a row, so Miss Barrow's cousin stopped by the Seddons' to find out what was going on. Seddon coldly told him he'd already missed the funeral; when the cousin came back the next day and asked about the will and insurance money, which was of course his real interest in the matter, Seddon said he knew nothing about any of it. It was at this point that the cousin began to grow suspicious, so he alerted the police, and before long the Seddons were in custody, held on a charge of willful murder. The trial was held in early 1912, and, though the jury declared Margaret innocent, Frederick Seddon was found guilty and presently hanged by the neck until dead.

"If Seddon had not given evidence himself," writes the editor of the trial transcript, who was himself in attendance, "few jurymen would have dared to bring in a verdict of guilty." He did, however, and so they did, because, although the case against him was entirely circumstantial, and not even *Law & Order* circumstantial, where it's obvious that the guy did it and the defense attorney is just grasping at straws, but actually circumstantial, Seddon was "as cold and hard as a paving stone, and had such a jaunty and overweening confidence in his sharpness and cleverness that, had the issue been less grave, it would have been only human to wish to triumph over him at any cost." The editor is of the opinion that "he was obviously capable of the crime with which he was charged" and that upon hearing his testimony the jurors' only choice was to believe he was "a scoundrel and a murderer." During his trial, the one moment of feeling Seddon permitted himself came when the prosecutor accused him of counting Chickie's gold coins in his office while his assistant watched. Seemingly unperturbed by the idea that he had murdered his tenant in cold blood for her money, he was nevertheless incensed to be thought such a "degenerate, greedy, inhuman monster" as to *count it in front of his assistant*. "I would have had *all day* to count that money!" he shouted at the prosecutor.

Here is what the editor of the transcript has to say about Mrs. Seddon and her relationship with her husband:

> His wife, as she appeared to those who saw her at the trial, is a somewhat more inscrutable character. A woman with some pretensions to good looks, dressed with some taste, apparently gentle, and rather weak in character, she had been doing practically the whole of the lighter household work of this fourteen-roomed residence, living, in short, the life of a domestic drudge. It was obvious from the evidence, and as a matter of knowledge outside the case, that she and Seddon were not on particularly good terms; it was obvious that everyone in his household was frightened of him, and that he was a hard and tyrannous man. Business, and especially Mr. Seddon's business, came first in that house, and every one had to make way for it. Looking at his wife as she gave evidence, it seemed humanly incredible that he would trust her with any matter of importance outside the kitchen, and, in fact, I am convinced that he did not. Only once did Mrs. Seddon unconsciously reveal the attitude in which they stood to one another, when to the question as to why she did not tell him something, she answered, "He never used to take any notice when I said anything to him; he always had other things to think of." And, again, "I did not tell my husband everything I done; he never told me everything."

Seven months after Seddon was executed (his last act was to summon his solicitor to the jail to find out how much his furniture had fetched at auction; when he learned it wasn't much he fell into a rage), a newspaper printed Margaret Seddon's statement that her husband had held her at gunpoint and forced her to do his dastardly bidding, but this statement was revealed in short order to be false, made for money and because Margaret was sick of her neighbors calling her a murderess. So she up and went with her five children to California, where one of those children married and produced offspring that married and produced offspring that married and produced me.

These, then, were the models of marriage my family put before me:

Two people who had an affair with each other, betraying the spouses to whom they'd promised to be faithful, and then went on to spend their lives working for the rights of the disenfranchised.

One woman who, after nine attempts, still couldn't seem to get it right, no matter how hard she tried.

A tyrant and adulterer and/or serial rapist who cowed his wife into such submission she helped him commit murder.

I didn't know what I was supposed to take from these examples. That you can have a successful marriage but only if you break one of the Ten Commandments? That the level of marital dysfunction in my family had been declining for a hundred years, so even if Mike and I had problems here and there I'd still probably make it through without being executed?

That marriage is a very, very complicated thing?

I finally received definitive word from my dad. No wedding rings anywhere. Not his, not my grandfather's, not my great-great grandfather's.

So I decided to leave Mike ringless for the moment and ignore the problem and hope it would go away, an approach that had always served me well in the past.

3

Deciding
on Living Arrangements

W e envision our ceremony," I read, "as being—"
"Tedious," Mike offered.

I glowered at him. "We envision our ceremony as being—"
"Full of bitterness."

"Sweetheart, this is the third question on the first page of the book. If you won't even let me finish asking it, how are we ever going to plan a wedding?"

It was early June of 2008; I was still in the doghouse with the Los Angeles branch of my family, but I had enough faith in my ability to regain my credit that I'd started buying wedding planning books (on this occasion I was reading from Karen Bussen's *Simple Stunning Wedding Organizer*). Mike rolled his eyes and sighed but pursed his lips, so I continued. "We envision our ceremony as being: short and simple, reverent and religious, non-religious but spiritual, secular and straightforward, formal and traditional, or unique and personalized?"

"Which one will annoy you the most?"

"One that involves you."

"I think it should be unique and personalized, and we should just speak our vows from the heart, rather than writing them ahead of time. And we can give each other rings we make out of wood we find in the park, since we'll be getting married in the cathedral of nature."

"Why are you so mean to me?"

"Because it's fun."

"I'm checking 'short and simple.'" I did so. "Next question. Our favorite time of year for our wedding would be (rank from one to five): spring, summer, fall, winter, doesn't matter."

"I don't know," said Mike. "What do you think?"

"I don't know. What do *you* think?"

"I asked first."

"No, actually, given that I'm reading the questions, *I* asked first."

"I don't know. Fall?"

"Sounds good to me." I opened my mouth to start reading but stopped short. "Wait a minute. *This* fall? As in like three to six months from now?"

Mike cocked his head. "I don't see why not."

I looked at the book under my hand. "Then I think we have to go through the questions a little faster."

But the next Thursday afternoon, when I got out of the summer-school class I was teaching—a class during which a homosexual college student thinner than I will ever be had referred to the heart-rending "Non, je ne pourrais jamais vivre sans toi" ("If It Takes Forever I Will Wait for You") as sung by Catherine Deneuve in *The Umbrellas of Cherbourg* as "the blonde girl's 'I'm sad' song," so my nerves were already frayed—I checked my messages to find one from Mike asking me to call him. His voice was unsteady; not all the way to the-house-is-on-fire unsteady or listen-honey-we-have-to-go-into-witness-protection-so-get-ready-for-a-new-life-as-a-Mennonite unsteady, but still worrisome. When I got him on the phone, Mike said, "My dad has cancer."

"Oh, sweetheart," I said. "I'm sorry."

"He went to the doctor last week because his asthma was getting worse, and it turned out it wasn't his asthma. It was a stage-four tumor."

"Oh, sweetheart," I said. "I'm so, so sorry." Silence on the other end of the line. "Listen, I'm going to jump in a cab right away. Is there anything I can bring you?"

"No. Just come home."

I had always loved being around Mike's parents. Mr. Combs was huge and his wife tiny, like the discarded first draft of a nursery rhyme; he wore glasses and was mostly bald, with a few wisps of hair floating perpetually above his head, while Mrs. Combs was thin and perky and usually dressed in something yellow. (Whenever I refer to them by their last names, people ask me why I hate them. I don't hate them. I love them. It just feels really weird and disrespectful to call them by their first names, and I obviously can't call them "Mom" and "Dad." Maybe it's a Southern thing.) Theirs was the first family I'd had a close connection to in which nobody had divorced anybody or died of a terminal illness or been hanged by the neck until dead for murdering his tenant. The nuclear unit was whole, and I found this incredibly comforting.

What made it even more comforting was how *ordinary* they seemed (as opposed to my family, which going back even just a few generations is made up, in addition to the real estate moguls, the civil rights activists, and the poisoners, of rednecks, Communist agitators, slave owners, horse thieves, and a pretender to the throne of Russia). Mike and I would visit them and we would sit around and they would say prosaic things about their neighbors or the beach or the choir they had recently joined and then we would leave, and I thought it was heaven.

"I read this great article the other day," Mr. Combs would say, "about ways to keep deer from eating your hosta plants."

"It's awful," Mrs. Combs would say. "We used to have beautiful hostas. Then the deer ate them."

"Apparently it's really hard to keep deer from eating your hostas," Mr. Combs would say. "You can put up strips of plastic bags. But then we'd have strips of plastic bags all over our front lawn. You can put a stick in the ground and put some soap on it, and sometimes that'll work, but not always. We're going to try it and see."

"That's great," I would say, thrilled at the *normality* of it all. "Good luck."

Then there were the occasional moments of surprise indicating that not all was as it seemed, which moments tended to happen on Christmas Day. Take for example Christmas of 2005, when we went to the firing range. Mr. Combs, as a member of the NRA, owned several guns, one of which I used to shoot at a poster of Osama bin Laden provided by the firing range for that very purpose. (For the record, I hit him in the face. Five times. The government should have just airlifted me into Afghanistan and *Zero Dark Thirty* would have been twenty minutes long.)

Or, going back earlier, the day I first met them, Christmas of 2003, when we (Mike, his sister, Cathy, my dog, Sasha, and I) drove a couple of hours to their small ranch house on the Jersey shore, where they had moved a few years earlier from Iowa. The whole thing was as traditional a Christmas as one could ask for: we talked about the weather, we ate hors d'oeuvres, we looked at embarrassing childhood pictures of Mike and Cathy, we ate Christmas dinner, we opened presents, we ate pie, we talked about real estate, we ate chocolates, we pulled out their homemade Ouija board and contacted their spirit guide, 28.

Mike had alerted me to the possibility that this might happen. Apparently it's 28's job to greet the recently deceased upon their arrival in the afterlife, but he's also very interested in the spiritual progress of those of us who have yet to shuffle off this mortal coil; at this point he'd been sharing his insights with Mr. and Mrs. Combs (and, through them, with Mike and Cathy) for almost three decades. 28's communications while I was there concerned themselves partially with the Combses' failure to talk to him in a while—it had been five weeks or so—but mostly with Cathy's path in life. He gave her what seemed to me to be a lot of good but self-evident advice, like "Cathy must consider the choices she makes in the upcoming months carefully." ("He's not so good with practical things," Mike had told me. "You'll ask him, 'Where are my keys?' and he'll say, 'They are where they need to be,' or, 'They will appear when you are ready for them.'" I thought this sounded obnoxious, but since there are already precious few supernatural beings in whose names countless civilizations have not been massacred, I felt it unnecessary to alienate this one.)

At one point, Mr. Combs asked me whether I had questions. Of course there were any number of things I was dying to know (Is whatever this thing is with Mike going to work? Or should I really not be dating him at all, but holding out for someone with straighter teeth? And in the meantime can you tell me which gym Chris Meloni works out at so I can go there and wait until he's there and then arrange a completely accidental meeting in the shower?), but somehow I couldn't quite see my way through to asking about them, so I said, "No, nothing in particular—though if 28 has anything to say to me, I'd be happy to listen." I hoped by this maneuver both to get some good if self-evident advice and to ingratiate myself with my hosts while also avoiding the awkwardness of addressing a cardinal number.

Unfortunately, 28 saw right through my ploy; he bade me welcome and told me to read the transcripts Mike's parents had made of his other communications with them so I could get to know him better. This didn't strike me as such an onerous assignment until Mike told me that these transcripts ran to some five hundred typed pages. Then 28 went back to castigating Mr. and Mrs. Combs for neglecting him, and eventually those of us who lived in New York piled into the car and went back there.

Of course I knew that the family had had its *contretemps*; Mike's father had been a drunk for years before sobering up, for example, which meant that Mike hadn't grown up in a particularly normal atmosphere, but Mr. Combs was now a teetotaler so I just reveled in the blandness. I spun daydream after daydream in which Mike and his family and I sat around for the rest of our lives *actually talking about the weather*. It was sheer bliss.

Until the esophageal cancer.

Which of course made wedding planning difficult.

I am no stranger to terminal illness. My mother's juvenile diabetes didn't kill her until I was nineteen, but I don't remember a day when I didn't know she was living on borrowed time; as the years passed, furthermore, the interest rate kept rising, and it became more and more difficult to act as if the grim and usurious reaper weren't hanging out on the porch, waiting for the right moment to slip in. I can still summon with perfect ease the image of my mother's legs, swollen, useless, flowery with scabs and bleeding ulcers, still hear her groaning in pain while I wrote my high-school senior-year report on Nikolai Bukharin and the Stalinist purge trials of 1938 because she'd been like this all evening and I'd already gone to her room a couple times and asked whether I could do anything to help her (my dad was off desegregating the University of Alabama) and been given a haunted "no" or just a shake of the head, and if I couldn't stop her agony then I might as well just write the goddamn report.

So when Mike, concerned about his mother's ability to care for a husband so much larger than she was, asked, "Can my parents move in with us when my dad gets too sick to take care of himself?" what I said was not "Are you insane?" but "Sure," because to be able to help his family deal with a slow death by illness and to refuse to do so seemed unconscionable. "As long," I added, "as I come first."

It ought possibly to have occurred to me that, having dealt with a dying parent once already, I didn't really need to repeat the experience.

Mike and I live in a three-story brownstone in Brooklyn the top floor of which we rent out to others; at the time, those others were Cathy and her husband Dennis. The two remaining floors are divided as follows: on the second floor are Mike's office, the TV room, the living room, a bathroom, and our bedroom; on the first, the dining room, my office, a bathroom, and the kitchen. The plan we made in anticipation of the Combses' arrival, sensible if discommodious, was that we would move everything in my office upstairs to the living room with the exception of the piano, which, since it couldn't go around the corners necessary to get it up the stairs, we would put in the kitchen. My in-laws-elect would take the dining room and my office as their apartment, putting me effectively in the middle of a Combs sandwich, and we would share the kitchen with them. Though this plan opened the door to all sorts of unnerving possibilities—I didn't know exactly what would happen to the piano if I accidentally flung spaghetti Bolognese into it, for example, but I felt confident that its sound quality would not improve—it seemed at least to allow Mr. and Mrs. Combs a sufficient measure of privacy and independence while at the same time not completely uprooting our lives.

And I'm sure it would have done exactly that, if we had stuck to it.

When I came home on the day the Combses moved in, however, I went to the kitchen to make some lemonade (I make delicious lemonade) and found the door shut.

"I thought we were going to leave the kitchen door open and close my office door," I said to Mike in Couplespeak.

(Permit me, please, a brief digression on the subject of Couple-speak, that dialect of English in which the second person singular pronoun is replaced with the first person plural. "We should be more careful about locking the front door," Mike might say, meaning, obviously, "You should be more careful about locking the front door." "We ought to clean up the kitchen more thoroughly when we cook" means "You ought to clean up the kitchen more thoroughly when you cook," and so on. Basic Couplespeak is pretty straightforward. It's when you add reciprocal pronouns that things start getting interesting. "We need to make more of an effort to hear each other's perspectives" actually means "You need to make more of an effort to hear my perspective"; notice that the singular ["perspective"] is also replaced with the plural ["perspectives"].

(Constructions more complex than these should be attempted only by the advanced student, because something like "Remember when we said we thought it was important to shut the gate before we go to bed?" actually means, "I resent you deeply for not shutting the gate before we go to bed even though I've asked you countless times, and your consistent failure to do so makes me feel like you don't think anything I say is important, so, while I was considering trying to find something we could watch together tonight, now I'm just going to turn the channel to HGTV and if you want to watch two hours of *House Hunters International* with me on TiVo you can, but if you don't then I don't give a damn.")

"I thought we were going to leave the kitchen door open and close my office door," I said to Mike in Couplespeak.

"There's no fan in your office," he said, "and my dad's really hot, so we needed the air from the kitchen to cool him off."

"Oh, okay," I said. "So we'll get some fans tomorrow and we can open up the kitchen again, right?"

"Absolutely," said Mike soothingly.

"Sure," he said when I asked again a few days later, and I felt a sinking sense of doom.

"Look," he said when I asked once more, a week after that, "my dad's got enough going on as it is. Can you make do without the piano for a few more weeks? Because that's how much time he has."

I took a breath and said, "Fine." Certainly if I were dying of cancer I imagined there would be things I'd rather do with my time than rearrange furniture. Besides, I didn't have any imminent deadlines, and if worse came to worse I could use the pianos in the department where I taught at NYU. As for the kitchen—well, we just ordered a lot of pizza.

If I had it to do over again, I would have left the house the instant I saw that closed door, bought twenty industrial-strength fans, come back, plugged them in, and posted armed guards to guarantee me access to the kitchen. Because, though I didn't understand it until it was far too late, by giving up the kitchen, we were giving up our hearth.

It had been our habit, Mike's and mine, to take some time every day when he came home from work to sit together in the kitchen and discuss whatever was on our minds. These minutes of connection grounded us and allowed us to direct our attention to each other, if only for a few minutes, so that we could keep our relationship on track and notice anything that needed to be addressed and share an intimate moment and remind ourselves and each other how important it is to make yourself vulnerable to another person so that he can respect that vulnerability and show you that you're safe.

Without the kitchen, we didn't have that time. And we didn't realize how badly we would need it.

"Could you come downstairs to the bathroom and give us a hand, please?" said Mrs. Combs on the phone the day after they moved in. When I got there I found her and the hospice worker (there on her daily half-hour visit) standing by the sink while Mr. Combs sat naked in a plastic chair in the shower. They had managed to get him into the chair and bathe him, but Mrs. Combs, as I've said, was a very small person, as was the hospice worker, and even after the weight he'd lost to cancer Mr. Combs had to be heavier than the two of them put together, so once they were done they couldn't lift him out of the chair back to his walker by themselves, and he was too weak to help them.

The moment I stepped into the room I was put in mind of the scene in Genesis—Mrs. Grossman taught a memorable Sunday school class back in 1980—when, after God finished drowning everybody who hadn't paid enough attention to Him, and the surviving pairs of rabbits and malamutes and South American giant anacondas were frolicking around in the corpse-enriched mud, Noah planted a vineyard. "When he drank some of its wine," according to Genesis 9:20-25, "he became drunk and lay uncovered inside his tent. Ham, the father of Canaan, saw his father's nakedness and told his two brothers outside. But Shem and Japheth took a garment and laid it across their shoulders; then they walked in backward and covered their father's nakedness. Their faces were turned the other way so that they would not see their father's nakedness.'"

I get it, the horror of seeing a parent vulnerable and helpless and impotent, the shock of that power reversal—I get it.

There I was, in the bathroom, pulling my fiancé's naked father up from the plastic chair he was sitting in, doing everything within my power to keep my head turned away; in that position, though, I had absolutely no leverage, so finally I gave up and looked at him, a man now seemingly made entirely of gray, spotted flab, hands trembling, eyes unfocused, and hauled him up. And I can't remember the last time I had felt so ashamed.

Oh, wait, yes I can; it was, funnily enough, when at the age of seventeen I had to help my naked mother get out of the shower.

Ha.

This is the problem when you try to be a caretaker to a dying family member: it can't be done.

A caretaker's job is to make a dying person comfortable as he fades. A family member's job is to try to accept that death is on its way and prepare to welcome it as sincerely as possible. As a caretaker, you're charged with his body; as a family member, you're charged with his soul.

When you try to do both jobs, though, the idea of comfort is replaced perforce by the idea of survival. When your father is dying, as Mike's was downstairs, it is out of human ken to remember, as you hold the bucket when he starts vomiting, that you're not trying to keep him alive. Every act becomes about wringing one more second of life out of the ruin in front of you. And if that's what you're doing then it's categorically impossible to prepare for death. You can either fight it or accept it. You can't do both. This is one reason people put terminally ill family members in hospice.

Adding to the impossibility of playing both roles is the fact that it becomes ever more difficult to compass the life fading while you watch, because when he loses control of his bladder or his bowels and you have to clean up the mess you are filled with hot, savage resentment.

Also, you suck at being a caretaker. You weren't trained for this; you've never done it before. Half the time all you succeed in doing is putting him in more pain than he already felt, like when you try to adjust the mystifying tubes sticking out of his nose and mouth because he's obviously in horrible discomfort and you end up stabbing something in his nose with something on the tube and he groans in what sounds like agony and you think, great, something else I've made worse.

And having a health-care worker stop by once a day for a half hour doesn't count as hospice.

I had known these things for a long, long time, having grown up with a mother who was dying before she even bore me. Mike had realized them, I think, fairly soon after his parents moved in with us. But his mother had not and did not. I brought to bear every blandishment of which I could conceive, but to no avail.

I understood the impulse; really, I did. I just worried that Mrs. Combs was robbing herself of something that would have been a great comfort to her, now and hereafter. And she was going to need all the comfort she could get. I kept hoping 28 would back me up, but the homemade Ouija board stayed out of sight.

"He should be all right," Mrs. Combs said as Cathy opened the door for the two of them to leave. "He's been sleeping well the last few days."

"Okay," I said.

"We'll be back in a few hours."

"Okay," I said, and the door shut.

I turned on the television and began watching a *Law & Order* rerun; it was the one where the murderer's lover says he can't testify against the murderer because they'd gotten married in New Paltz back when the mayor of New Paltz was marrying same-sex couples (like my friends Rob and David) and therefore the spousal-privilege exception applied. So Sam Waterston gets the New York Supreme Court to declare marriages of same-sex couples invalid, a process which takes all of two minutes—would that the judicial system moved as quickly in real life—and then he comes back and puts the lover-whoops-husband on the stand and says, "What conversation did you have with the defendant on the date in question?" And the lover-whoops-husband says, "I'm not going to answer that," and Sam Waterston's bushy, bushy eyebrows shoot up and he asks the lover-whoops-husband what he thinks he's doing. And the lover-whoops-husband is like, screw you for invalidating my marriage. And Sam Waterston throws him in jail for contempt of court and says he'll keep him there as long as he wants, and then the murderer, who despite being a murderer is actually kind of a decent guy, confesses so that the lover-whoops-husband won't have to languish in jail forever.

I turned the TV off and called my father, who is a lawyer. "Dad," I said, "I think *Law & Order* just cheated," and explained the setup. "But once a jury is empanelled," I said, "doesn't Sam Waterston have to keep the trial going, and if a witness doesn't give him what he wants then it's just too bad? He can't put the trial on hold indefinitely, can he? And just make the jury sit there for months and months?"

"Joel," said my father after a long silence, "I'm sorry to say this, and I hope you don't take it the wrong way, but you have a fine legal mind."

"How could you say such a horrible thing?" I said, and then Mr. Combs started making choking noises and I said "I have to call you back" and hung up and went over and tried to figure out what was going on, but of course I had no idea what was going on since I'M NOT A DOCTOR and I thought, well, okay, he's choking on something, maybe I should turn his head, so I did and he started vomiting so I grabbed a nearby bedpan and held it under his mouth while he vomited into it and kept vomiting, there wasn't even that much of it, it just seemed so vivid, and I wanted to call Mrs. Combs but my cell phone was on the table and I stretched as far as I could but I wasn't able to reach it without pulling the bedpan away from Mr. Combs's head, which would mean that he would be vomiting on the rug, and I *loved* that rug, but he just kept right on vomiting, so finally in between bouts of vomit I leapt for the phone, grabbed it, leapt right back to hold the bedpan under his mouth, and called her.

"Um," I said when I got her voice mail, "could you please come home? Because Mr. Combs is vomiting and I'm not quite sure what I ought to do." Shortly after that he stopped vomiting and went back to sleep and I turned the TV back on and watched another episode of *Law & Order*. When Mrs. Combs called back she was deeply apologetic; she said from what I described it sounded as if he had been vomiting not food but bile, which was something he'd been doing a few days earlier and which, while not pleasant, at least meant there wasn't now yet another food he would refuse to eat anymore. Then she hung up and came back home, which I appreciated but which was also hideously, hideously unfair, because you never think that "for better or for worse" means "even if you're going to be trapped in your son's house taking care of a stinking puking mass of insensate flesh that used to be a person who cared about you."

Then I spent the rest of the day trying to figure out exactly what part of this situation it was that the Defenders of Traditional Marriage found so threatening.

Meanwhile, Mike and I began, hearthless, to ignore each other. Only a little at first, but then more and more, rejecting each other in turn—well, if *he's* not going to pay attention to *me* then *I'm* certainly not going to pay attention to *him*—until we might as well have been just two roommates in one apartment. (Well, two of four roommates in three-quarters of an apartment, really, but you get the idea.) He would come home from the hospital and we would say hi and then I would go back to working on my computer in the living room (where, if you'll remember, we had relocated my office) and he would sit down in the TV room and we would spend the evening as isolated from each other, he in front of the television, I at my desk, as if we were lab rats in cages.

Oh, how I came to loathe that television. It was a sixty-inch flat-screen high-definition TV that took up the whole wall. The room we had installed it in was actually full of things we'd bought even though we knew they were too big for it. Sometimes this turned out to be a boon, like when we were draped over the vast decadently burgundy sectional sofa watching *Law & Order: SVU* and Chris Meloni took his shirt off, but even gazing in wonderment at Detective Stabler's larger-than-life abs couldn't make me forget that the television was my rival for Mike's affections. I would come into the TV room after a while, hoping to talk about Mike's day or my day or, you know, the old person dying below us, and he would just continue to stare blankly at the TV watching his goddamn home and garden shows, *House Hunters* and *House Hunters International* and *Flip This House* and *Flip That House* (I'm not making that up, those really are two different shows) and the rest of them. And I felt that I'd never understood true loneliness before.

I assumed my experience dealing with terminal illness would come in handy as Mr. Combs deteriorated. When his blood relatives found themselves emotionally unmoored, I thought, I would be able to help them find ways to handle what was happening.

I thought wrong.

Apparently, Protestants don't deal with death by continually making morbid jokes about it.

Jews are not like this. The closer somebody is to death, the funnier Jews are about it. People have been killing us for millennia, so we're used to the idea; it's a well-known joke that the answer to "What's the meaning of [any given Jewish holiday]?" is "They tried to kill us, we won, let's eat."

(I must point out that I do not speak for the entire Jewish people. I'm sure there are hundreds of thousands of Jews, millions of Jews, who don't react this way. I just don't know them.)

My mother was Episcopalian, but she'd been married to a Jew for decades, so her pseudo-Anglican sensibilities had been blunted beyond repair. And when she was dying, our house might as well have been the set of a really good Lisa Kudrow picture. It was unthinkable that any of us should ask whether anybody wanted anything from the drugstore and not be answered with, "Some morphine or a casket, whichever's cheaper." My favorite moment came a few days after she died. My father was talking about the snazzy new car phone he'd bought a few months before (this was in 1992, before cell phones). Our exchange went something like this:

> MY DAD: I was just so glad to have that phone, because it meant that your mom could reach me no matter where I was—at the office, on the way home, wherever. It really was a lifesaver.
> ME: Well, not quite.

Now, given that Mike's parents had a spirit guide named 28, one could argue that they ought not in fact to have been classified as Protestants, but Mike says that people in the Midwest are Protestant no matter what religion they are, so within a few hours of their arrival, I learned that the way I could best help would be to *keep my mouth shut*. I don't recall the attempts at humor I made—doubtless the Combses' appalled reactions have led me to repress the memories—but I do remember that when Mr. Combs said he'd spent his whole life working and being busy and now what was he good for, I bit my tongue before the word "fertilizer" rolled off it, and realized I had a difficult time ahead of me.

"So how should we do this?" I said, looking at Mr. Combs. "Should I take his left side and you take his right side?" Mr. Combs was uncomfortable in the bed the hospice had given us, so we had decided to try to move him back to his own bed. "Then his weight would be divided evenly between us."

"No," said Mike, "because he'd just fold up at the middle and we'd drop him."

"That would be bad."

"Here, you take his feet and I'll take his shoulders."

"Won't he still just fold up at the middle and we'll drop him?"

"No, because if we carry him with our arms out we can keep him straight."

Thank God Mr. Combs was asleep during this conversation, because in his position if I'd heard two people talking about me like this I might have died of powerlessness and shame.

I went to the foot of the bed and Mike to the head. I put Mr. Combs's feet on my shoulders and stretched out my arms underneath his legs, while Mike burrowed his arms underneath his father's back. "One," Mike counted, "two, three!" and we lifted and *moved* as fast as we could, and we had enough momentum to get him over the metal rail of the hospice bed and we were going to be okay and then I tripped on the leg of an armchair and lost my grip and Mr. Combs folded at the waist just like we'd been trying to avoid and there he was hanging from us, his ass on the floor, my face growing red with the effort not to drop him, even though I'd already dropped him, and Mike said "Step back!" and he stepped forward and we were able to maneuver into a position from which we could deposit him in the armchair.

"I know we've had other things on our minds lately," I said to Mike as we caught our breath in the kitchen, preparing to move Mr. Combs from the armchair to the bed, "but do you want to get married in Connecticut on Tuesday?" By now Connecticut had joined Massachusetts as a marriage-equality state. "Because then your dad could be there."

"That's sweet, but he can't take a train."

"No, I looked it up, it's only an hour-long drive, and if you apply for a marriage license you get it the next business day, so we'd only have to be there for two weekdays. We could do the legal stuff there and then have a ceremony later on here, when things have calmed down and we have time to plan."

"Could you get the license and then my folks and I come up after work the next day and get married?"

"No, we both have to be there to apply for it."

"Joel, I can't miss two days of work right now. The Joint Commission on the Accreditation of Healthcare Organizations is coming to the hospital at the end of the week, and I'm the only one on my unit who knows how everything is organized. If I skipped two days, we could lose our accreditation."

"Fine," I said huffily. "How about the next Tuesday?"

"That's Christmas week. Look, tell you what: what if we go on"—he looked at the calendar on his iPhone—"Monday the fourth of January and get married on Tuesday?" He didn't have to say, "if my dad is still alive."

"Okay. That sounds good." I didn't have to say it either.

Mr. Combs died on the morning of December 26, protected to the last by the Defenders of Traditional Marriage from the horror of attending his son's wedding.

"What happens when he dies?" my friend Sarah had asked. "What's Mike's mother going to do?"

"She'll stay with us for a few months, on the top floor, and then she'll find her own place."

"Really?"

"Well, that's what Mike says."

"And has Mike told her this?"

"I'm not sure," I said. "I guess I should check with him."

When I checked with him, he said, "Well, we haven't discussed it explicitly, but I'm sure that's her plan."

Then Mr. Combs died, and Mike and his mother began discussing her move upstairs. "I'd like to wall this doorway up," she said when they were checking out the space as Cathy and her husband prepared to move to their new place a few blocks away, "and I want to extend the bathroom by moving that wall further out."

"Those are not the words," I said to Mike when he reported this conversation to me, "of someone who is planning to stay with us for a few months."

"Hmm," he said.

We hired somebody to do the work on the upstairs apartment; in the meantime Mrs. Combs stayed in the suite she'd been sharing with her husband. She stayed in the suite she'd been sharing with her husband for half a year.

And by the time she had been living in her suite on her own for a month or two I realized that, when I'd thought before that I'd never understood true loneliness, *that* was when I hadn't understood true loneliness, because now I would have *welcomed* seeing Mike and myself as two lab rats in cages, because at least lab rats can look at each other through the bars but by now I was virtually invisible to him, and he to me. The reason you get into a relationship, ultimately, is to create a space on earth in which you're accepted and celebrated for being yourself, but to do that you have to allow your partner to see you being yourself, and eventually we were showing each other virtually nothing. Each tiny rejection, unacknowledged, forced a tiny retreat—oh, okay, I guess I can't show him *that* part of me either—and eventually I felt I was living in an opaque shell I had constructed of myself, full of emotion, of anger, sorrow, and longing on the inside, but unable to let any of it out, because he wasn't letting any out either, and so the only result of expressing these feelings would be the discovery that, though I was physically only a few feet from my TV-watching fiancé, I was in fact, in the vast emptiness of the world, alone.

I began to fantasize about selling the television on Craigslist one day while he was at work. "Perfect for single man or woman," I would write in the ad, leaving out "pernicious and destructive for couples." Mike would be beyond furious when he got home to find it gone, but at least I would have gotten rid of that bitch. I actually sat down one day and started drafting a post, but then I realized that, since the only thing Mike liked more than watching his goddamn home and garden shows was looking on Craigslist for furniture we couldn't afford to buy, he was almost certain to come across the ad and foil my plan before I could execute it. I considered charging like ten dollars for the TV, so that somebody would snap it up right away, but then I saw that I had ninety-three cents in my checking account, so I thought better of it.

I tried to find solutions. We went to a couples therapist, but our session didn't get off to a great start.

"I'm furious," said Mike when the therapist asked him how he was feeling. "Joel sprang this appointment on me *yesterday.*"

"But, Joel, you made this appointment with me three weeks ago," said the therapist.

"And your point would be?" I said. I'd waited so long to tell Mike because, though he'd agreed in principle to the idea of couples therapy, that had been months ago. If I asked him about it now, I knew he'd say it wasn't a good time, so I figured that, rather than having a fight, it would be easier not to give him a choice in the matter.

I thought the therapist was lame and Mike liked her, which I put down to his having spent much less time than me on the couch, but in the end he said he was simply too busy to do couples therapy. (Mike swears up and down that he never said this, and that the reason we didn't continue couples therapy was that I failed to fulfill my promise to look around for other therapists I liked better. I had made such a promise, it's true, but only before Mike said he was too busy to do couples therapy at all. Mike is *crazy*.)

One evening I said to him, "Look, could you just turn off the fucking television for five minutes and talk to me?"

Jaw clenched, he answered, "Joel, I just spent ten months watching my father die. Has it not occurred to you that I might need a little bit of time to be alone with my thoughts and feelings and not make entertaining you my highest priority for every minute of every day?"

"I watched my mother die for twelve years," I said, "and you know what? I didn't have to become a cloistered monk; I just lived my goddamn life, because there was nothing else I could do, so why can't you just fucking grow a pair and *deal with it?*" I stormed downstairs to ask Mrs. Combs whether I could come into ~~my~~ her kitchen to pour myself a glass of Diet Mountain Dew but then I heard her sobbing, presumably about her dead husband (God, what was *wrong* with these people?) so I went to the corner store, invincible in my lack of compassion, and bought half a dozen candy bars and came back and ate them in ~~the living room~~ my office while I read *The Count of Monte Cristo*, a 1,100-page novel about revenge.

The next day, I ransacked Mike's office until I found the transcripts of 28's conversations with his parents; if Mike and I couldn't even talk to each other about the fact that we couldn't talk to each other, I thought, maybe 28 would have some advice.

The transcripts, I saw when I found them, covered the period of time from November of 1977, when the Combses first made contact, through August of the following year, just before Mike's tenth birthday. The conversations were fascinating.

28 had been born in England in 1053, it turned out, and had been murdered at nineteen, though the transcripts also contained conversations with other entities, mostly other students of 28: Yaew (communicating from the future, in the year 4276), Norm (a really obnoxious six-year-old), Baird (a Prussian who died in 1865), Pistils (a trucker), Jacob (from Lubbock, Texas), and so on.

28's advice was usually metaphysical in nature and, in some cases, surprisingly consistent with the most advanced science of the day, science Mr. and Mrs. Combs could have known nothing about (the many-worlds interpretation of quantum mechanics, for example), but just as often he gave them personal advice:

> 28: Ken [Mr. Combs] is angry at himself for not doing those things that he often thinks or wishes he would do. He knows he should drink less. He tells himself he will, but doesn't, then feels as a failure to himself. He gives himself headaches and colds. If he stopped feeling that he has failed, he would not have these things. If he did as he believes he should, he would also not have these things. He can trust himself and his world.

He shared his thoughts on their marriage:

> 28: You celebrate eleven time years but you feel the 11,000 other time years it is especial [28 had apologized early on for a slight lack of facility in English]. You have gone here in love and are having a triumph. Marriages are made in heaven. They are pre-planned, as are all relationships. Yours is one of breathtaking expansion.

He offered his insights about their children:

> 28: Mike must know that there is plenty for all. He need not be pushy or be afraid of not getting his share.

which Mike had apparently found comforting and which I thought was particularly penetrating, though now whenever I remind Mike that 28 says he need not be pushy he gets really annoyed, which upsets me; how else can it be felt but as a blow to one's self-esteem to be trusted less than the product of 7 and 4?

I discovered early in the transcripts that 28's advice did not confine itself to the emotional.

> 28: In other times and places you will not have physical existence. Use it now, now. Find joy in what you are experiencing now. Have fun, have fun. Do it. Yes.
>
> MR. COMBS: Let's take a break.
>
> 28: No. Go to bed now. You have physical bodies. Use them.
>
> MRS. COMBS: Go to bed?
>
> 28: Yes. Have, if I may intrude, sex. You have a body. Use it for experience and for joy.
>
> MR. COMBS: Good night.
>
> 28: Bye, luv. Bye bye.

(Throughout the transcripts there were many, many occasions on which 28 suggested that Mr. and Mrs. Combs use their bodies for experience and for joy.)

After I finished all the transcripts, I really didn't know what to make of them. Mike's childhood was so dysfunctional that at one point he stopped speaking to his parents for a year. After Mr. Combs died, Mrs. Combs seemed absolutely, utterly incapable of action without him. "We always worked as a team," she said to Mike when she asked him to make the funeral arrangements. "I don't know how to do anything on my own." What that meant, as far as I could tell, after Mike spent half an hour explaining on the phone to the funeral parlor whatever she could not explain because she could not pick up the phone, was that her husband had been happy to make all the decisions and she had been happy to disclaim responsibility for any of them.

How reliable could a spirit guide be who called this marriage one of breathtaking expansion?

At the same time, what wouldn't I give to find out, via independent verification—even by my subconscious, if that's what 28 is—that Mike and I have gone there (wherever there is) and are having a triumph? I don't know the answers to anything, and I don't think Mike does either, but if somebody else claims to, what would be the point in stopping our ears?

I think the idea of True Love is one of the most insidious inventions ever to issue from the demonic forges of the human mind. As far back as Plato with his sphere-people who got broken in half and spent their lives seeking the half-sphere-people from whom they'd been separated, the thought has existed that if we could just find the right person, the person whose edges protruded where ours receded, the person with whom we fit perfectly, we would be whole. We would no longer suffer the agony of being alone.

The problem is that this is bullshit.

The agony of being alone isn't situational, it's existential; it's an agony that comes as a free gift with being alive. True, having a boyfriend or a husband or (one presumes) a wife means that you have somebody to talk to about that agony when it gets too awful to bear. It also means, however, that, if your fiancé gets into a snit because you ate the last of the chocolate ice cream or were late for dinner or forgot to put the recycling out and stops speaking to you, you have nobody to talk to and as far as things stand at that moment *you never will*. If the two of you kiss and make up, then you're back to having somebody to share the agony with; great, except that it's horribly easy to miss something when you kiss and make up, horribly easy to be so relieved that he's speaking to you again that you ignore the twinge of resentment you feel that you're *always* the one who has to take the recycling out and why can't *he* take the recycling out every once in a while and then he gets *mad* about it on top of everything, Jesus *Christ*, and then you forget that you ignored the twinge of resentment but it's still there and then the next time you fight there's another one and you start to build up emotional plaque and if you're not careful then you're trapped in that opaque shell you've created, just as surely as Madeleine Usher buried alive in the sepulcher. You're in just as much pain as everybody else but forced to pretend you're not, because otherwise you'd have to admit that your marriage is a failure and that you're not worth loving, so you go on day by day, with no hope of ever sharing the unbearable burden of being alive, because if you don't talk about it with anybody then at least you're the only one who *knows* that your marriage is a failure and that you're not worth loving. And you start daydreaming, and you think, *well, what if he had an epiphany and renounced all fleshly connections to become a priest, I couldn't very well be expected to stay in this marriage* then, *could I?* and when you see inspirational pamphlets on the sidewalk you consider picking them up and leaving them strewn about your house, as subconscious advertising. Or you think, *what if I could provoke him into hitting me? Not hard at all, but just enough that I could immediately leave him and everybody would be on my side and I would be single and full of hope again?*

Of course, it's entirely possible that I'm just a bitter, cynical man who wants everybody else to be as frightened of life as I am. I mean, I *am* a bitter, cynical man who wants everybody else to be as frightened of life as I am, but it's possible that my attitude toward True Love comes not from any insight on my part but from an unconscious effort to spread my misery as far and wide as I can.

Yet I don't think so.

Mike's mother finally moved upstairs, and we took back our kitchen and regained much of our equilibrium, but when we get into fights with each other—usually because Mike is being completely unreasonable—I find myself back in that lonely, lonely place. In fact, I don't know any couples in whose relationship this dynamic doesn't operate at least occasionally.

The sphere-people were a myth. I don't think the mystery of human character can be contained in three dimensions; each of us protrudes and recedes in directions physicists have yet to imagine.

Or what if this is just what marriage is?

Mrs. Combs lived upstairs for a year and a half or so, joining the block association and having dinner with us once or twice a week, but she never really seemed to be at home in the neighborhood and finally she moved to New Jersey. I observed to Mike not long afterward that it had been largely his enthusiasm for the idea that had led her to move upstairs. "I think if she'd been left to her own devices she would have just moved out to Jersey pretty soon after your dad died."

"You're probably right," said Mike.

"Why was it so important to you that she live with us?"

"I don't know." He paused for a long time. "I guess I thought she might become the mother I always wanted her to be."

"And how did that work out?"

"Look," he said, hearing resentment that hadn't been in my voice except that it totally had, "I'm still really upset about how unsupportive you were that whole time."

"Well, *I'm* still really upset about how you let your parents take away our kitchen for nine months."

"Joel, what was I supposed to do?" His voice was getting heated. "My father needed that door open."

"Oh, grow *up*," I said. "Your *mother* needed that door open."

He was silent for a few moments. "You're right."

"She needed a sense of control over her situation."

"You're right."

"You *knew* this!" I shouted. "You *knew* this! You asked me to let your dying father move into our house and I said he could on *one condition*, that you put me first, and you *promised* you would, and you broke your promise *the very first day*! And you wonder why I wasn't more *supportive* when he died."

"*Yes*, I *do*, because *I needed you and you weren't there.*"

We sat, staring at each other in silence.

4

Dealing with
the Legal Business

The first same-sexers to wed in California after the state Supreme Court's decision in favor of marriage equality, I understand, were Del Martin and Phyllis Lyon, activists who had been together since 1952—fifty-six years—and the mayor of San Francisco himself performed the ceremony. I spent a lot of time crying that day too, not because I felt a further shift in civil rights but because the sight of two ancient lesbians getting hitched made me almost unbearably happy.

I don't know what it is about old people that I find so compelling, but put one onscreen and I'm mesmerized. Be one and say something moderately wise-sounding and I'm eating out of your hand. Maybe it's aspirational. Since my thirties have been so much better than my twenties, maybe I'm hoping that my life will get better and better, decade by decade, until I'm so far from the man who used to ask his psychiatrist boyfriend about overdose effects of different prescription drugs so he'd know what to use when the time came to kill himself that I won't even recognize him. Or maybe it's the other way around; maybe I feel somehow that a face filled with lines and wrinkles is, ultimately, the result of Michelangelo chipping away at the marble, trying to get rid of anything that doesn't look like a horse, and who we are at seventy or eighty, battered by the slings and arrows of outrageous fortune, is as close to our true selves as we're going to get. And the idea of being in that position with Mike at my side makes me think that someday I might not be afraid of anything.

In any case, Martin and Lyon weren't the only same-sex couple to marry that day; hundreds of others married with them, and hundreds the next day, and the next. My family in Los Angeles had not forgiven me—this was before Mike's parents moved in with us—so I couldn't join them yet, but the day was coming soon, I knew, when I would.

And then Mike's parents moved in with us and things started winding up for the 2008 election and all of a sudden everyone was talking about Proposition 8, the ballot initiative put forward by ProtectMarriage.com to amend the California state constitution with the addition of the phrase, "Only marriage between a man and a woman shall be valid or recognized in California." But I wasn't worried. "This is never going to pass," I told Mike.

"Why?"

"Because it's so badly written as to be virtually meaningless."

"It's so cute that you think people are going to notice."

Let's say we analyze the structure of the sentence "Only marriage between a man and a woman shall be valid or recognized in California" as "Only [[noun] [prepositional phrase]] [predicate] [predicate adjective] [prepositional phrase]." We could then create an analogous sentence that read, for example, "Only Sam over there is good in bed." It's perverse to read this as indicating that Sam is good in bed when he is over there but not when he is anywhere else; the reading of this sentence must be therefore that Sam, who is over there, is good in bed, but that nobody else is. (Note that such an assertion, were I actually to make it, would be libelous; I happen to know from personal experience that, while Sam certainly is a sexual dynamo, he is by no means the only one in the world. Or the only one in New York. Or in his immediate family.) If we apply this structural understanding to our original sentence, we see that the only possible reading of Proposition 8 is therefore that a marriage between a man and a woman is valid or recognized in California, but that *nothing else* is. Not a marriage between two women or two men, of course, but also not felony statutes, not stop signs, not the law of gravity.

Actually, it's a little more complicated than that, because in addition to the "only" problem we also have the issue of "or" (valid *or* recognized) and whether it's exclusive or inclusive, as well as the issue of whether "in California" applies to "valid or recognized" or only to "recognized," and when it all adds up the thing ramifies so many times that I don't have the heart to continue this, because no matter how you interpreted it Proposition 8 didn't mean what its proponents said it meant.

To do that, the law would have had to read something like, "In California, a marriage is valid only if it is between a man and a woman." But it didn't. So instead, it meant that, within the state borders, all felony statues were unconstitutional and one could go on a killing spree without fear of any consequences.

After the election one had half a mind to do so, though it might have been difficult given that by then the law of gravity was neither valid nor recognized in the state.

But, as I say, the wretched grammar wasn't the only reason for my lack of concern about the upcoming vote on Proposition 8. The No on 8 folks were raising tens of millions of dollars to spend on publicity, and besides, thousands of same-sex couples had already gotten married, and thousands more would get married before the election. The citizens of California were not going to unmake what turned out by November 4 to be 18,000 marriages. No way.

Except: way.

After John McCain conceded the presidential election to Barack Obama—the Prop 8 vote was still being counted—I called my dad to rejoice with him. When our initial effusions of happiness had spent themselves, I asked him how he felt.

"You know how people say, 'I never dreamed I would see something like this in my lifetime'?" he said.

"Sure," I said.

"Well, *I did*," he said. "*I did* dream I would see something like this in my lifetime. And then there came a time when I stopped dreaming, because things changed. And tonight I'm dreaming again. I'm so excited about the future, and so full of hope. And, Joel, you've got a great country ahead of you."

So when I went to bed on the night of November 4, I too was full of hope, because the United States had just elected a black president and because enough votes remained uncounted in California for me to believe that Proposition 8 might be defeated. But over the next few days, as the dust from the election settled, it transpired that the measure had passed with just over 52 percent of the Californian vote. Not an overwhelming majority, but enough to put marriage once again out of the reach of any same-sex couples who didn't live in Massachusetts or Rhode Island.

"I don't get it," I said to Mike. "How could this happen?"

"I don't know, babe."

"I'm going to get to the bottom of this."

Part of how it happened, the Internet revealed over the next few days, was that members of the Church of Jesus Christ of Latter-Day Saints had given twenty million dollars to the Yes on 8 campaign (even though Mormons make up less than 2 percent of the population of California). The Internet was soon filled with pictures of Mormons going to temple on Sunday, November 9, in the face of crowds of hundreds and in some instances thousands of protesters.

"That suits me fine," I told Mike, "given the hypocrisy of an attempt to define marriage as the union of one man and one woman by a sect whose founder took twenty-eight wives."

"You are a very angry person," he said.

But then same-sexers were presented with additional targets for our anger, one in particular: "The same voters who turned out strongest for Barack Obama," read *The Washington Post* on November 7, "also drove a stake through the heart of same-sex marriage. Seven in ten African Americans who went to the polls voted yes on Proposition 8."

"That's disappointing," said Mike.

"Yeah," I said. "But there's a strong Christian tradition in the black community, and religious people tend not to vote for marriage equality, so I guess I can understand."

As this piece of data disseminated itself throughout the blogosphere, however, it seemed that there were a lot of people who disagreed with me (which I think is the real problem with the world, but that's for another book).

"Many gays and lesbians worked hard to elect the first African American president," I read in somebody's comment on Queerty .com, "only to have African Americans betray us by voting against our equality in droves." And I thought, *You are a bad person with a small penis.* Then I wrote in response, "Are you seriously suggesting you voted for Obama out of empathy for black people rather than because his record on LGBT issues was better than McCain's and therefore more likely to benefit you?"

"You actually left that comment on a website?" asked Mike when I told him about this.

"No," I said, "I just typed it and then didn't send it. I may have a lot of bad ideas but I still know better than to get involved in an Internet discussion about politics."

As time went on, though, the commentary seemed to me to get worse. "Hoodwinked," read somebody else's comment. "Bamboozled. By blacks. They, as an oppressed group of people, showed absolutely no empathy and had no problem doing to us what was done to them." And I was like, *You are a VERY bad person, and not only do you have a small penis but your clothes make you look fat.* And this time, after I had clicked through to the commenter's own blog and read a few posts to find out a little about him, the comment I typed with trembling fingers and didn't send read, "Yes, marriage equality is an incredibly important issue. But you typed this comment in your office at your job, which brings you five or six figures a year, or from your computer, which you own, in the living room of your house, which you own, and which you've had the education and experience to get a decent mortgage on rather than something that's going to leave you homeless and ruin your life, or maybe from your smartphone, which you own, on the way from your doctor's office, where you can go because you're insured, or maybe having just left for a massage at the spa, which you can afford, and you're seriously comparing yourself to a whip-scarred slave picking cotton in the field wondering whether massa is going to be in the mood to rape her tonight?"

By now I had learned, from other, less popular websites, not only that the 70 percent figure quoted by *The Washington Post* was wildly inaccurate to begin with—and that any racial distinctions in Prop 8 voting patterns virtually disappeared when you asked about religion rather than race—but also that the black population of California was so small that in fact if *every* registered black voter in the state had voted *against* Prop 8 it *still* would have passed. (A convincing study done in 2009 by the International Humanities Center makes it pretty clear, by the way, that the only way Proposition 8 could have passed, given the statistics reported, was by means of election fraud, so really, no matter how many Californians voted against it, of no matter what religion and race, we'd have lost anyway.)

I had also learned, however, that Equality for All, the organization in charge of the No on 8 campaign, hadn't done itself many favors in the black community. Of the dozens of TV spots they produced in the months leading up to the vote, not one targeted black people, portrayed a black couple, or ran on black TV stations. Black lesbian Jasmyne Cannick wrote an op-ed piece in the *Los Angeles Times* suggesting that Equality for All's "occasional town-hall meeting in Leimert Park—the one part of the black community where they now feel safe thanks to gentrification—to tell black people how to vote on something gay [wasn't] effective outreach." (Equality for All didn't seem to have done much better with other communities of color; in a state where 17 percent of the voting demographic is Latino, for example, they produced exactly one TV spot in Spanish.)

This depressed me. Maybe "Equality for All" really meant Equality for All Whites, I thought spitefully. Or perhaps the No on 8 campaign had simply assumed, because blacks and Latinos are seen as less likely than others to be sympathetic to gay political aims, that they were a lost cause?

And I was like, what harm could energetic outreach have done, given that, only a few decades ago, calls to protect "traditional marriage" from "activist judges" determined to open it to "a population incapable of moral development" came from people trying to ban marriage between not same-sex couples but mixed-race couples? Did it not occur to anybody in the No on 8 campaign to point this out to black Californians?

In 1957, Virginia residents Mildred Jeter and Richard Loving went to Washington, D.C., to get married, since as an interracial couple—she was black , he was white—they were forbidden to marry by the state's Racial Integrity Act of 1924. (Laws like this one, by the way, forbade marriage not just between whites and blacks but also between whites and Asians, whites and Latinos, and so on. In fact, between 1875 and 1943, the immigration of Chinese women was so severely restricted that Chinese men in America were essentially forbidden to marry at all.)

Shortly after the Lovings' return home they were arrested—police invaded their house hoping to interrupt them having sex but had to be content with using the marriage certificate on the wall as grounds to charge them—and convicted, their jail sentence suspended as long as they promised to leave Virginia for twenty-five years.

It took a decade, but eventually the Lovings ended up before the Supreme Court, which in 1967 ruled that anti-miscegenation laws violated the U.S. Constitution: The freedom to marry, wrote

Chief Justice Earl Warren, had "long been recognized as one of the vital personal rights essential to the orderly pursuit of happiness." Marriage was one of the "basic civil rights of man."

The ruling needed some time to propagate—in fact, it seems to be propagating still, given that in 2009 a judge in Louisiana refused to marry an interracial couple, though at least after the story spread around he was forced to retire—but for all intents and purposes laws forbidding mixed-race couples to marry were dead in this country.

I'd always been aware that, after my parents moved to Jackson, Mississippi, to do civil rights work with the Lawyers' Constitutional Defense Committee, one of the earliest cases they worked on resulted in the first legal interracial marriage in the state, but I'd never known any of the details, so at one point in college I made my father tell me the whole thing.

It was 1970, and Roger Mills, who was white, fell in love with Berta Linson, his black coworker at the NAACP. The week before their wedding they applied for a marriage license, but Mississippi's anti-miscegenation statute, even though *Loving v. Virginia* had been decided three years earlier, was still on the books, and the county clerk denied their application.

The wedding was scheduled for Sunday, but when my father went to the local judge on Tuesday morning to ask for a hearing, the judge—a staunch segregationist who did not scruple to call black people "niggers" and "chimpanzees" from the bench—looking over his schedule, allowed as how, with some pending naturalizations and a golf tournament, he couldn't see scheduling the hearing before Thursday afternoon; this meant, according to my father, that he would issue an order late Friday afternoon denying the marriage license, and the wedding would be off.

Immediately, my father called the appeals court—essentially the judge's boss—and explained to them what was going on; after hearing the muttered cursing on the other end of the line, he was not surprised to get a call in short order from the judge's secretary telling him that a hearing had been scheduled for early that afternoon. "In the meantime," my dad told me, "just in case, I called the U.S. Supreme Court and let them know what was going on, and they said, Justice Marshall has the papers, if necessary— meaning if we had gotten nothing down below, we would have gotten some kind of an order from the Supreme Court." (I think many of the problems in this country could be solved if it were still possible to say, "And then, just in case, I called the U.S. Supreme Court and let them know what was going on." Then again, that would require a U.S. Supreme Court that actually believed in the Constitution, so I guess it's not that simple.)

"Well," my dad told me, "the local judge issued an order the next day, on Wednesday, in which he said something like, 'I would have preferred to let the ordinary process of the law take its due course'—meaning that the Mississippi state court would take its time and finally review the thing and say, it's reversed, long after the wedding was supposed to happen—'but these people are planning a big interracial display of their romance this Sunday'— he actually used the words 'a big interracial display of their romance,' it's right there on the piece of paper—'and the appeals court told me, in no uncertain terms, that if I did not issue this order, they would.'"

And that Sunday my parents attended as big an interracial display of romance as Jackson had seen in a long time.

        The plaintiffs (at least one of the couples) have planned a big interracial display of their romance in a big church wedding to be attended by many guests from within and outside of Mississippi. It may be very well doubted that any irreparable injury would be done either of these couples by a more orderly and deferential disposition of this matter here with more judicial orderliness and respect for our brethren on the state bench to whom this matter has been submitted and where it is now pending disposition. This court has no disposition in any case to shirk, or evade its duty here regardless of the nature of the case, but does not approve of inordinate haste in the disposition of any case where judicial proprieties are cast to the winds on such a flimsy pretext such as is presented here.

Several days after the Proposition 8 vote I was contemplating this story and a thought occurred to me. "Could Roger Mills and Berta Linson," I asked my dad when I got him on the phone, "have just had the wedding ceremony that Sunday and then gone to a state with no anti-miscegenation law to get legally married the next week?"

He thought for a while. "Well, I guess they could have," he said.

"But the idea never crossed their minds. Or any of your minds."

"No."

"But Mike and I decided to get married out of state and then have the ceremony in New York. Why were we okay with something that you found unacceptable in 1970? Have we become so inured to our oppression that we can't even see we're accepting second-class citizenship?"

"Gee. I don't know."

We talked about it for a while until we realized that same-sexers had decoupled modern legal marriage and ceremonial marriage (more on this later) by inventing the commitment ceremony in the late twentieth century; in 1970, without such a precedent, the idea never even occurred to my father and his colleagues and friends. (Of course American slaves had their own kind of commitment ceremony, but it had been a century since anybody had had to jump the broom instead of speaking vows.)

But that raised another question: why hadn't interracial couples invented the commitment ceremony before *Loving v. Virginia*? My father and I supposed it must have been that there weren't enough interracial couples for the idea to have gained critical mass, but it turns out that one in every twelve American marriages is now between people of different races, so maybe it was something different. Maybe the fact that many northern states had abolished their anti-miscegenation laws in the nineteenth century showed southern interracial couples that what they wanted to do was possible—just not where they lived. Whereas same-sexers could find no example of other same-sexers speaking wedding vows anywhere on earth, so there was a void in imaginative possibility that we filled with the commitment ceremony.

Or maybe Mike and I had become so inured to our oppression we couldn't even see that we were accepting second-class citizenship.

In 1996, Eric Zorn wrote a brilliant column in *The Chicago Tribune* in which he listed a bunch of appalling things opponents of marriage equality for same-sex couples had said and then revealed that they had actually been said by opponents of marriage equality for interracial couples. Since he pretty much owns that trick I can't repeat it here, but if you haven't seen the column, which is worth reading, I've posted it on my website at joelderfner.com /zorn. In the meantime, let's consider some comparisons.

Sexuality-Based Objections to Marriage Equality	*Race-Based Objections to Marriage Equality*
"Support traditional marriage. Children must be raised with morals and principles." —California Senator Roy Ashburn, press release, 2005[1]	"The social status of the children is bound to be low, their educational opportunities poor, and their moral background bad." —W. M. Castle, *Biological and*

---

1. Shortly after saying this, Ashburn was arrested for drunk driving with a charming young fellow he'd picked up at a local gay bar in the passenger seat.

Sociological Consequences of Race Crossing, 1926

"The law of our state protects and preserves the sanctity of marriage between a man and a woman."
—Alabama Attorney General Troy King, 2004[2]

"The sanctity of . . . marriage and the home shall be upheld. . . . Miscegenation (sex relationship between the white and black races) is forbidden."
—*Production Code of the Motion Picture Industry,* 1930

"Aware of the social stigma of living with homosexually-behaving adults, school-aged children generally suffer stress associated with their shame, embarrassment, [and] fears of peer rejection."
—George Rekers, *A Rational Basis for the Arkansas Regulation,* 2004[3]

"The progeny of a marriage between a Negro and a Caucasian suffer not only the stigma of such inferiority but the fear of rejection by members of both races."
—John Shenk, California Supreme Court, *Perez v. Sharp* (dissent), 1948

"In every society, the definition of marriage has not ever to my

"A man can not commit so great an offence against his race, against

2. Shortly after saying this, King was discovered by his wife, we are told, in bed with a charming young fellow who, after joining King's staff nine months earlier as an unpaid intern, was now earning $57,504 a year, because, according to King spokesman Chris Bence, the young fellow—only a few years out from being crowned homecoming king of a local university—was "indispensable in terms of the many functions he carrie[d] out in th[e] office."

3. Shortly after writing this, Rekers was discovered on vacation with a charming young fellow he'd picked up on rentboy.com. Rekers explained that he'd hired the young man to help him with his luggage because of his recent surgery, which excuse held water until a photograph surfaced of Rekers struggling with a bunch of suitcases while the charming young fellow stood indolently and suggestively by.

knowledge included homosexuality. That's not to pick on homosexuality. It's not, you know, man on child, man on dog, or whatever the case may be. It is one thing."
—Sen. Rick Santorum, AP interview, 2003[4]

his country, against his God, in any other way, as to give his daughter in marriage to a negro— a *beast*—or to take one of their females for his wife."
—Buckner Payne, *The Negro: What Is His Ethnological Status?*, 1867

And it goes on and on—priests who refuse to perform interracial marriages will be arrested, if we allow interracial marriages we might as well allow incestuous ones, you name it.

And I thought, if Equality for All had handed something like this table or Eric Zorn's column out in black neighborhoods, the black vote in California would have split very differently than it did.

But when I emailed a friend of mine who works for an LGBT-rights organization about this question, he wrote back, "Honestly? Every bit of opinion and messaging research the LGBT organizations have ever done has shown that using civil rights movement imagery and comparisons in trying to talk about same-sex marriage to black people only backfires. And I've seen that happen time and time again myself. A lot of black people react badly when white same-sexers try to compare gay rights to civil rights. They think, 'Oh, really? When was the last time

4. Rick Santorum has yet to be discovered, as far as I'm aware, with a charming young fellow he picked up anywhere. I just wanted the opportunity to say that I could very easily have populated the left column of a much longer list like this entirely with the words of people who were later revealed to be in same-sex relationships of one kind or another, and if I had any problems populating the right column with people who were later revealed to have been in interracial relationships of one kind or another I suspect it would be only for lack of access to less reputable—which is to say more honest—sources.

anybody tried to keep *you* out of a voting booth?' And that's why that kind of argument wasn't used in the Prop 8 battle."

And I was like, oh, my God, I'm an *idiot*. Because how could it be any other way? If a group of Christians showed up at my house to tell me how their exclusion was identical to mine as a Jew, it would be all but impossible for me to listen to anything they had to say, because all I would be thinking was, right, because you can't turn around without hearing somebody talk about how this is a Jewish country founded on Jewish principles and come December you can't take a step without hitting a menorah or go shopping without being confronted by store employees dressed as Maccabees and your grandmother refused to tell you a single story about her childhood ever because all her friends were slaughtered in concentration camps? If a bunch of heterosexuals came to talk to me about how they experienced the same diffi-culties I did as a gay person, I'd slam the door in their faces but not before saying, "Of course, because politicians regularly compare your relationships to bestiality and incest, and you grew up believ-ing that you would never be permitted to marry somebody you loved, and anywhere except Manhattan, and even sometimes there, you have to think carefully about what it might cost to hold your boyfriend's hand!" How could a mass of white people descend upon black neighborhoods saying, "We're suffering the same injustice as you," and expect to be granted a listening ear? (Or, as I saw it expressed on one black same-sexer's blog, "If your rapist were raped and came to you asking for help, how do you think you'd respond?")

So I realized that my oh-we're-all-being-oppressed-together point of view had been a little naïve.

Still, I thought, aren't we all being oppressed together?

By a few weeks after the victory of Proposition 8, the racist comments online were out of control. "It was niggers," read a comment I saw on Towleroad.com, "yes that's right I said it, niggers who voted for Obama on one hand and then on the same goddamned ballot voted to erase a fundamental human right for an entire class of citizens. The day every black person in America is singing 'free at last' is the very same day that millions of ignorant homophobic Obama-voting niggers vote to keep gays as third class-citizens."

It could be pointed out that the Internet has never been the first place to turn for coolheaded, rational discussion. But the racism wasn't just online. Apparently, at a Los Angeles gathering one protester shouted to a black gay couple: "The niggers better not come to West Hollywood if they know what's best for them." One would think that the "No on 8" signs the couple was carrying would have earned them some measure of immunity, but evidently one would be wrong.

When I read about things like this I am appalled at the selfishness of white gay men. I think white gay men should fucking *know better*.

Disenfranchised people will never get anywhere oppressing other disenfranchised people, especially after we all saw *Milk* and, if we stopped drooling over Dustin Lance Black at the right moment, we all heard Sean Penn as Harvey Milk say, "Without hope, not only gays, but the blacks, the seniors, the handicapped, the *us*-es, the *us*-es will give up. And if you help elect more gay people, that gives a green light to all who feel disenfranchised."

How can it be anything but crystal clear that outsiders are all the same in our exclusion? It's one thing to be fighting against people in power who are stepping on us, but if we're stepping on each other then what are we but their creatures, doing their miserable work for them while they laugh at us all because as far as they're concerned we will never be *us* and always be *them*?

And don't even get me started on white gay guys who won't sleep with black guys or Asian guys but insist they're not racist, because they fucking are.

"I don't see how I can write it," I said to Mike before I started working on this book. "I'm so aware of my privilege as an upper-middle-class white man. Talking for hundreds of pages about how oppressed I am seems an act of effrontery so brazen it defies measurement."

I mean, do same-sexers really need another book enumerating our woes as the population 3.4 times as likely as others in America to have an annual household income exceeding $250,000, the population twice as likely as others to have graduated from college, the population 77 percent of which "believe[s] in indulging [it] self"? (I suspect those numbers might turn out very differently if broken down by sex, race, and income, but all that would do would be to make the advantages even starker in the populations I'm talking about.)

The time I felt this most sharply was in the lead-up to the 2008 presidential election. That year 861,664 families were foreclosed out of their houses, despite a moratorium on foreclosures. Twenty-two thousand Americans died because they didn't have health insurance. One out of every ten black kids had a parent in prison (as opposed to fewer than two out of every hundred white kids). And it seemed like, wherever I looked online, the only thing white gay men could talk about was Hillary or Obama, who's better for the gays—or, as I came to think of it, HillaryorObamawhosbetterforthegays. Some of the commentary was remarkably insightful and thought-provoking; some of it was pro-Clinton, some pro-Obama, a very little pro-McCain. But none of it ever addressed anything except HillaryorObamawhosbetterforthegays. A report is released showing that more than one out of every six children in America lives below the poverty level? The next day the gay blogosphere is all, HillaryorObamawhosbetterforthegays. A tsunami kills 78,000 people in Burma? HillaryorObamawhosbetterforthegays.

Back in my dating days, I spent a particularly unfortunate evening with a fellow who'd just been to his first Log Cabin Republican meeting; when I got home, I added to my online profiles the sentence, "You don't have to be political, but if you are you should lean to the left." A month or two later I got a funny response to one of those profiles that included the sentence, "I'm a Republican, but that doesn't mean I don't know how to stand up for my rights." I wrote the guy back and wished him luck but said I thought we probably weren't right for each other. What I wanted to say was, "I don't give a damn if you can stand up for your rights. I want to know whether you can stand up for *other* people's rights."

This, by the way, is why I find the Log Cabin Republicans so contemptible. It's not that they're so deluded they think their party cares about them, though they are. But at least the guy talking about Obama-voting niggers wasn't betraying what he thought of as his own people. Log Cabin Republicans, as I see it, in order to enrich themselves at the expense of the poor, are perfectly willing to sacrifice not just outsiders but their own brethren.

In any case, what Mike eventually said in answer to my question about how I could write this book was, "Just because the battle for marriage equality benefits you doesn't mean it isn't worth fighting."

"Watch this, honey," I said to Mike, and pressed play on the computer.

"Atlanta native Demetria Mills wants what many women in their thirties want," said Tom Brokaw. "To marry the person she loves."

"It's an important transition in life," said the woman with light brown skin who appeared on the screen. "It's an important way of becoming a family."

"One man standing in her way," continued Brokaw, "is

Pastor William Sheals." He asked a dark-skinned man in a fire-and-brimstone beard about his refusal to marry Mills and her partner.

"It's unacceptable," said Pastor Sheals, "it's ungodly, and it's unnatural." Comparisons to forbidding an interracial couple to marry, he continued, were irrelevant. "Being born black is not a sin nor a choice."

"It just drives me *crazy*," I said, "all these people who think we choose to be gay."

"Well, to be fair," Mike said, "there's strong research, but nobody's actually *proven* we don't."

"Why are you like this?"

"Because it makes you love me."

"But seriously, doesn't it drive you crazy?"

"I just don't like framing the argument in those terms. If we *did* choose to be gay, would it be okay to say we couldn't get married?"

"No."

"Exactly. We don't choose our sexuality, but that's irrelevant."

And he was right. So after that conversation, I'm reluctant to make the standard but-you're-wrong-homosexuality-isn't-a-choice objection, because it leaves room, however implicitly, for the idea that there's something wrong with homosexuality. Like, if being gay were a *choice*, we'd *definitely* choose otherwise, but it's not, so we're *stuck* with this *defect* and can't you just let us get married because you feel *bad* for us?

But being gay isn't a defect, not any more than it's a choice.

If it were a choice, however—if we just woke up one day and said, *Gee, that Barbra Streisand sure has a great voice, I think I'll go have sex with an attractive man and hope nobody beats me to death or anally rapes me with a toilet plunger on my way home!*—I suspect that Eric Zorn would have been able to write almost the same article, comparing marriage discrimination toward same-sexers to marriage discrimination toward people, for example, who have chosen different religions.

Sexuality-Based Objections to Marriage Equality	Religion-Based Objections to Marriage Equality
"Support traditional marriage. Children must be raised with morals and principles." —California Senator Roy Ashburn, press release, 2005	"Throw into this devil's brew of modern culture the fact that persons of different religious . . . background marry and have children and you have situations in which the children of these relationships . . . grow up with little or no spiritual/moral instruction/ guidance." —comment on kendallharmon .net, 2007, on the dangers evil Catholics hold for good Protestants
"The law of our state protects and preserves the sanctity of marriage between a man and a woman." —Alabama Attorney General Troy King, 2004	"You must either annul this marriage or trample underfoot all our maxims, upsetting this section of our law and removing from marriage the sanctity of the sacrament to which it has been raised." —M. Jamme, 1783, on the dangers evil Protestants hold for good Catholics
"Aware of the social stigma of living with homosexually-behaving adults, school-aged children generally suffer stress associated with their shame, embarrassment, [and] fears of peer rejection." —George Rekers, *A Rational Basis for the Arkansas Regulation*, 2004	"It would be a bad idea to marry a woman who is not properly Jewish, in which case your children would be stigmatized and would themselves be unable to marry Jews." —Rabbi Shraga Simmons, *Legitimate Conversion*, 2005

"In every society, the definition of marriage has not ever to my knowledge included homosexuality. That's not to pick on homosexuality. It's not, you know, man on child, man on dog, or whatever the case may be. It is one thing."
—Sen. Rick Santorum, AP interview, 2003

"Those who have relations with Jews or animals . . . are to be buried in the earth alive, while their possessions are taken for evidence or the public good."
—French legal code, thirteenth century

I could go on (you should see some of the things people have said about marrying Zoroastrians), but I won't. I'll just say that people all over the world have been using marriage to marginalize minority groups for thousands of years—Egypt, Greece, Mesopotamia—and the arguments, down to the individual words they use, are always the same.

The day after I showed Mike the video of the Tom Brokaw interview, I watched it again. And this time, halfway through, I sat bolt upright in my chair.

"Dad," I said when my father answered the phone, "what was the last name of the guy you represented in the Mississippi miscegenation case?"

"Mills," he said. "Roger Mills."

"That's what I thought you said."

And two minutes with Google proved my suspicion correct: Demetria Mills, the Atlanta woman with light brown skin whose desire to marry her girlfriend Pastor Sheals had called unacceptable, ungodly, and unnatural, was the daughter of Roger and Berta Mills, the couple whose marriage my father had helped make possible in the face of opposition from people who thought it was unacceptable, ungodly, and unnatural.

Talk about destiny weighing heavily on a family's shoulders.

Demetria Mills worked, according to the Internet, in the Civil Rights Office of the Department of Education, as did her father, so I looked up her number and called.

"Hello?" she said.

"Is this Demetria Mills?" I said.

"Yes."

"Demetria Mills, the daughter of Roger and Berta Mills?"

"Are you a telemarketer?"

"No!" I said, and we had a long conversation about her work, my work, her parents, my parents, her fiancée, my fiancé, civil rights, marriage equality, and Jane Austen.

"Pastor Sheals bristles," Tom Brokaw had said, "at the suggestion made by Mills and others who compare the struggle to legalize same-sex marriage to the fight for civil rights," followed by Sheals telling us that he was "appalled by comparing the two. Apples and oranges."

There's something in this: it's very difficult to make comparisons. In many ways, black people and (white) same-sexers have little in common other than the circumscription of our liberty. Each group can lay claim to advantages the other doesn't share and obstacles the other doesn't face. Black people, for example, in contrast to most same-sexers, are except in rare cases unable to avoid violence and discrimination by remaining in the closet. And much of black America, unlike most of same-sexer America, is still bound by the transgenerational poverty that keeps the evils of slavery alive and well today. Same-sexers, on the other hand, cannot expect a politician who compares them to animals to be called to account for it, which for the most part black people can. Black parents aren't likely to kick their kids out of the house for being black, and those kids aren't likely to be bullied into suicide because they're black. Same-sexers can almost never lean on the rock of the church, which has sustained the black community through so much, for support, moral or practical.

(Of course, being black and being a same-sexer are hardly mutually exclusive. When I asked black same-sexers about their experience at the intersection of these two groups, they tended not to think in such a binary way. "I just think the whole discussion is so old-fashioned," said one. "I'm like, check your watch." Another said that as a rule he experienced more overt homophobia than overt racism but also that he never knew how to respond to white gay mens' appropriation of the persona of black women. "Can't black women," he said, "have their own identity?")

In *The New Yorker* in 1993, Henry Louis Gates warned against establishing "a pecking order of oppression. Measured by their position in society," he went on, "gays on the average seem privileged relative to blacks; measured by the acceptance of hostile attitudes toward them, gays are worse off than blacks. So are they as 'oppressed'? The question presupposes a measuring rod that does not and cannot exist."

What it comes down to is this: analogy is at the center of human cognition. In these matters it may be an inexact tool but it's still the best one we've got, and we have to use it, keeping in mind as we do that "compare" and "equate" mean two very different things.

"The only times comparisons to the black civil rights movement do seem to get any foothold with the black community," my friend at the LGBT organization had written me, "are when the messengers themselves are black. But those messengers are REALLY hard to find, sadly." One of the most persuasive such messengers, I think, is Mildred Loving, who said on the fortieth anniversary of the Supreme Court decision that bears her name:

> My generation was bitterly divided over something that should have been so clear and right. The majority believed that what the judge said, that it was God's plan to keep people apart, and that government should discriminate against people in love. But I

have lived long enough now to see big changes. The older generation's fears and prejudices have given way, and today's young people realize that if someone loves someone they have a right to marry.

Surrounded as I am now by wonderful children and grand-children, not a day goes by that I don't think of Richard and our love, our right to marry, and how much it meant to me to have that freedom to marry the person precious to me, even if others thought he was the "wrong kind of person" for me to marry. I believe all Americans, no matter their race, no matter their sex, no matter their sexual orientation, should have that same freedom to marry. Government has no business imposing some people's religious beliefs over others. Especially if it denies people's civil rights.

I am still not a political person, but I am proud that Richard's and my name is on a court case that can help reinforce the love, the commitment, the fairness, and the family that so many people, black or white, young or old, gay or straight, seek in life. I support the freedom to marry for all. That's what *Loving*, and loving, are all about.

As Mr. Combs grew sicker the election and the Proposition 8 vote gave way to other concerns; after Mike's father died and his mother finally moved upstairs, although we could have married legally in Connecticut and Massachusetts (the law there had changed to allow same-sex couples to marry even if they lived else-where), Mike and I, by unspoken agreement, had put our plans on hold. The damage done to our relationship by his parents' moving in with us and our months-long failure to deal with it healthily was going to take some time to repair. I still really wanted to go to couples therapy, but Mike was still too busy, so we figured we'd just let things rest for a while.

But then, in April of 2009, the Iowa Supreme Court ruled that same-sex couples could not constitutionally be kept from getting married. I tried to keep this information from Mike, but he found out somehow and started teasing me with the idea of having our legal wedding in his home state. "It'll be great!" he would say. "We can send out invitations on cornhusks."

It wasn't that I found Iowa objectionable as compared to the other forty-nine states. But when my father was a child, his parents, in an exception to the Eastern-Europe-to-New-York-to-Los-Angeles migration pattern of immigrant Jews in the twentieth century, spent a few years in Davenport, Iowa, and stories of his boyhood there, each more torturously wholesome than the last, were a staple of my youth, so I developed something of an allergy; when Mike discovered this, he joyously exploited that allergy as a way to tease me, and in the end I couldn't get married in Iowa because I knew that upon crossing the state line I would have a seizure.

In the months after the Iowa Supreme Court decision, though, I was rescued by Vermont, New Hampshire, and Washington, D.C., which joined Connecticut, Massachusetts, and Iowa as places where same-sexers could legally marry, along with the sovereign nation of the Coquille Indian Tribe in Washington State and Oregon, as long as one member of the couple was Coquille. Neither Mike nor I is Coquille, but I was pleased to have as many alternatives as I did, especially because it made it easier for me to put my foot down and say absolutely no way was he dragging me to Iowa for a wedding. "It would be so much easier," I said, "to do it on the east coast." Then I pulled out the big guns. "Easier and *cheaper.*"

"That's true," said Mike thoughtfully, his grandparents' Depression-era attitudes toward money, passed along in an un-broken line, coming to my aid, and I thought I'd dodged a bullet.

Then the reality TV people called.

5

Dealing with
the Legal Business,
Take Two

"Take a look at this link," said the email from my friend Sarah. "It's a reality show looking for straight women and their gay male friends."

"Are you and your friend the real Will & Grace?!" read the website to which the link took me (I quote it verbatim). "Are you a gay guy living with your straight best girlfriend? Are you a straight girl whose best friend happens to be gay? Do you finish each other's sentences? Have you already forwarded them this flyer and are on the phone freaking out? Gay guy and straight gal 'couples' who have outgoing personalities, active work and social lives and most importantly......a super close relationship. Couples from all walks of life are encouraged to apply including professionals, creative types, and executives. Roommates are a plus but not necessary."

"Should we go?" she wrote.

"I don't know," I answered. "I don't like the punctuation of this announcement. Also, we're not roommates."

"Thank God."

It was 2007, and the show, we found out when we arrived at the audition, would be, unsurprisingly, about friendships between straight women and gay men and was to be called *Girls Who Like Boys Who Like Boys*. The audition basically involved us gossiping with each other on camera about the guy Sarah had gone out on a couple dates with who had been an amazing kisser but who, she had discovered, refused to open a bank account because he was certain that in the coming world collapse everyone was going to go back to the barter system, so that was that for him.

"Do you have any questions about the show?" the guy running the audition asked when we were done.

"Are we going to be voted off?" Sarah asked. "I don't think I could handle that."

"No. There won't be any voting."

"Are we going to have to live in a house with other people?" I said.

"No, you can stay in your own house."

"Good, because I hate other people enough already without having to live with them."

But afterward, though we waited for our phones to ring, we kept hearing nothing, so we had to assume the producers had made the bizarre decision not to use us. When I got a call in January of 2010, therefore, I was surprised to hear the voice on the other end of the line identify itself as that of the director of *Girls Who Like Boys Who Like Boys*.

"Yeah," she said, "the project took a while to get off the ground, but it's been picked up for next season, so I'm calling some of the people who were interviewed to see what's up and try to figure out the right couples to cast. We'll be shooting from February through April." We talked for a while, and when I mentioned that since my previous interview I had gotten engaged her ears perked up (at least such was my telephonic impression). "Congratulations!" she said. "Have you set a date for the wedding yet?"

"We've tried a couple times," I answered, "but we keep having to cancel. So our plan is to do it at some point this year."

"Would you be willing to get married on camera?"

"Gee," I said, thinking quickly. They hadn't chosen the couples yet, and the opportunity for them to shoot a gay wedding would have to weigh heavily in our favor. "If we could do it without interfering with the actual wedding ceremony, I don't see why not. I mean, I'll have to ask Mike about it, but I'm sure he'll be fine with the idea." We talked some more and it gradually became clear that if they could film my wedding then Sarah and I were all but guaranteed to be cast. When the director and I hung up, it was with the understanding that I would talk to Mike and she would call me back in a few days.

Now, I am as red-blooded a narcissist as any who ever sat transfixed by his own reflection, so I found the idea of being on a reality TV show more thrilling than just about anything short of elevation to the nobility, and even then the decision would be a tough one in the case of anything less than a marquisate. In addition to the fifteen minutes of fame vouchsafed me by Mr. Warhol, however, I had an additional reason for wanting to be on the show, which was that, as a writer and composer, I will never make any money from my work if people don't know my name. (Mind you, I will probably never make any money from my work if people *do* know my name, either, but why not add a nauseating uncertainty to the equation?) I figured that, while I was unlikely to reach the heights of glory achieved by Khloe Kardashian or Bethenny Frankel, being on my own reality show couldn't hurt my chances in bookstores.

So the next day I told Mike about what had happened. "She even said they'd be interested in filming the wedding," I said carefully.

"Oh, God," he said. "What a terrible idea."

"I *know*, right?" I said immediately.

Crap.

"What did you tell her?" he asked.

"Well, I didn't want to say no without checking with you. You know, in case *you* were into it."

"I'm not."

"Good. Me neither."

"I just think a wedding isn't something that should be scheduled by a production company."

"*Exactly.*"

I spent the next couple days trying to think of some argument that would persuade Mike to see the situation differently, but I came up empty. I'd been with him for long enough to know all the nuances of all his tones of voice, and in this case those nuances left me no room to maneuver. So when the director called again and asked whether I had talked to Mike about the idea of filming the wedding, what came out of my mouth was, "Yes, and he's absolutely on board with it."

It was like watching myself push myself off a bridge.

But I realized after hanging up that the situation wasn't really so difficult. After all, he hadn't actually refused to *get married* on reality TV. He just didn't think the wedding should be *scheduled* for reality TV. So all I needed to do was schedule the wedding for reality TV without letting him know that that was what I was doing.

"Hey, honey," I said the next day as we prepared dinner, "I think we should have a spring wedding. Why don't we get married in April?"

"This April?"

"Yeah."

"That's less than three months away. Do you want me to chop the peppers?"

"No. But we can do something really informal, we don't have to—"

"Joel, I have my board-certification exam in May, and I'm going to need all my energy to prepare for that. I can't get married in April."

"I don't know, I guess I just feel like April is the right time."

"Well, you're wrong. And would you either chop the peppers or give them to me?"

Back to the drawing board.

"We want you to be one of the couples we follow!" said the director the next time she called.

"That's so exciting!" I said.

For a month I tried to come up with a way to guarantee my appearance on reality TV while not making my fiancé leave me, which would eliminate the reason for my appearance on reality TV in the first place, but since I lose my movie ticket between the window and the ticket-taker the logistics of such an endeavor were beyond me.

"Maybe this wasn't the best choice you've ever made," said my therapist.

"Fuck you," I said.

Finally I gave up. I wrote Mike an email confessing my duplicity and apologizing and telling him that I would do whatever he wanted me to do, and I sent it to him one morning shortly after he left for work. "In all of this, the most important thing to me is you," it read. "I'd rather respect you and your feelings than do the show." When he came home that evening he didn't say anything about it during dinner and he didn't say anything about it during *Project Runway* and finally I couldn't take it anymore and said, "Sowhatdidyouthinkaboutmyemail?"

"Oh, did you send me an email?" he asked. "I haven't checked since yesterday." (Mike is one of those maddening people who don't need to check their email more than once a day, and sometimes not even that, whereas if I can go the whole five minutes at which I've set my mail program without checking manually at least once I consider it a triumph.)

"*Yes*, I sent you an email, and you have to go into your office and read it now, but I'm going to stay right here so I don't have to be there when you do."

He raised an eyebrow suspiciously. "What have you done?"

"Just go check your email." He left the room and though I saw and heard Tim Gunn saying, "Make it work!" the only thing I could take in was the pounding of my heart. After a few minutes, Mike came back.

"Well, I knew *something* was going on," he said exasperatedly, "because you were being so weird about it." I realized I was holding my breath but I couldn't let it go yet. "I mean, I'm annoyed," he went on, "but I can see why you did what you did."

"Okay," I said, "but if it means forcing you into anything you don't feel comfortable with, then I'm not doing the show. Partially because such a beginning can't possibly be good for a marriage, but mostly because you need to come first."

"Well, if we just did the legal stuff for the cameras and then had the ceremony later on, would that give them what they need?"

"Probably."

"Okay. Then as long as it's the smallest, quietest, lowest-key event possible, let's do that."

I inhaled deeply, breathing for what felt like the first time in weeks. "It will be the smallest, quietest, lowest-key event in the history of time. Compared to this event, amoebic cell division will be like Y2K." What had I done in a past life, that I should go unpunished for such a crime in this one?

What I didn't take into account was that Mike, mental health professional though he be, sometimes has trouble knowing what he's feeling in any given moment.

And what he was feeling in this moment, it turned out, was rage.

"Sweetheart," said Mike, "it'll be fine. It's not that big a deal."

"You don't know me at *all*!" I cried, frantically pulling things out of cupboards and drawers. The camera crew was on its way over for the first morning of filming the two of us together, and I had realized that my plan to make us breakfast on camera had a fatal flaw, which was that if I did it my usual way, then America would know I made waffles from a mix.

"Then just make them from a recipe," Mike had said.

"*No*," I had responded—why was this so *difficult* for him?—"because the whole point of this is to make America think that

I'm a brilliant cook, and what kind of brilliant cook doesn't know the recipe for waffles off the top of his head?"

"Okay, honey," he'd said, giving up. "How can I help?"

I'd paced back and forth like a tiger in a cage. "That's it!" I said finally. "All I need to do is divide a bunch of waffle mix among the flour, the sugar, and the cornmeal and then pretend I'm measuring out the quantities by memory when in fact I'm actually just reassembling the right amount of mix!"

There was a brief pause. "If that will make you happy," he said.

So now I was scrambling to gather the materials for the perpetration of my fraud, apportioning the mix in easily memorable amounts between the sugar, the cornstarch, and the flour, finishing the job just as the camera crew walked up to our front door.

I was able, in the event, to measure a cup from the actual box of waffle mix while the cameraman was changing a battery or something, though I made sure to block my action from view with my body so that the director wouldn't see what I had done either.

"So," I said to Mike once the cameras were finally rolling and we sat eating breakfast in the dining room, where we had never, ever eaten breakfast before but where the light, according to the crew, was better, "where should we do the legal stuff?"

"You need to give the audience some context," said the director. "Say, 'No matter where we have the ceremony, New York State doesn't allow same-sex couples to marry, so we have to do the legal stuff somewhere else.'"

"Okay." I turned to Mike. "No matter where we have the ceremony, New York State doesn't allow same-sex couples to marry, so we have to do the legal stuff somewhere else."

"So where should we do the legal stuff?" asked Mike. He was incredibly stilted and even terser than usual, which is saying something.

"I don't know," I said, almost as stilted as my fiancé. "It would just be great to have just one wedding." *Oh, Jesus*, I thought. *With lines this sparkling, I'm sure to win an Emmy.* "What's your impulse?" A moment passed before a smile touched the corners of

Mike's lips and a you-owe-me glint shone from his eyes. I don't know how I didn't see it coming, but I didn't.

"Iowa."

"Oh, God," I said, because he had won. Americans make fun of Germans for expressing volumes with a single word—my favorite example these days is "Weltschmerz," which means "the mental depression or apathy caused by comparison of the actual state of the world with an ideal state." Well, that's nothing; in English all it takes to say, "You lied to and about me and manipulated me into going on this damn television show for you and believe me you're going to be paying for it for a long time but let's start with this" is one four-letter word spelled I-O-W-A. I knew I was beaten, and he knew I knew.

"You're going to make me do this in a cornfield, aren't you?"

"Barefoot."

"Oh, God." I had a sudden thought and eyed him suspiciously. "And what are we going to wear?"

"Overalls." Okay, he was actually kind of brilliant in front of the camera. "Or those tuxedo T-shirts. That'd be good."

The crew finally finished filming our breakfast and left. "Crap," I said, walking back into the kitchen, as Mike began to relax again. "I've completely forgotten how much waffle mix I put in the flour, sugar, and cornmeal."

"Then baking," he said supportively, "will be an exercise in hope."

We didn't talk about what had happened, but later that day he sent me a link to an online clothing store that sold overalls and tuxedo T-shirts.

Reality shows, it turns out, are just as staged as everybody thinks they are.

Girls Who Like Boys Who Like Boys seemed to be fairly conservative in this regard, in fact; most of the scenes the director staged were reenactments of events that had actually happened or at least enactments of events that hadn't actually happened but could have. We weren't directed to throw drinks in each others' faces, for example, or to talk smack about each other to common friends (there was always the possibility that we'd be *edited* to throw drinks in each others' faces or talk smack about each other to common friends, but there wasn't much I could do about that at this point). What all this meant, if I understood my friend who worked in the TV industry correctly, was that *Girls Who Like Boys Who Like Boys* was not a reality show but a docu-reality show, which is to say that it wasn't fake enough to be a reality show.

Within those parameters, however, it seemed like anything went. One Wednesday, for example, Sarah and I went to see my friend Ted Kadin, an Orthodox gay ex-rabbi calligrapher (I'm not making that up), to talk about a ketubah, the Jewish wedding contract. Ted is a serious scholar and had all sorts of things to say about Jewish traditions of marriage, but during a break in filming, the director said to me, "I met this guy at a bar last night who I think would be great for Sarah. He was reading a book. I got his number."

"That's terrific! What was the book?"

"I don't remember. Something smart."

"I'm sure she'll appreciate it."

"No, I need you to tell her you met him at a party and gave him her number, so then we can film them on a date together. He said he'd be fine with it."

"Um . . . okay."

Probably the most striking example I can give happened the day I showed up where and when they'd told me to and asked what we were going to be doing, and the assistant director said, "You're taking Sarah to a matchmaker, because you want her to be as happy in love as you are."

"Well, aren't I nice?" I said. "And I have good instincts. Sarah has actually been to a matchmaker before."

"Yeah, this is the same matchmaker. But we thought it would add a nice element to your storyline."

The sign on the matchmaker's door said "Club VIP Life," which made me think I was going to walk in and find myself face to face with Eliot Spitzer, but no such thing came to pass. The matchmaker interviewed Sarah, asking the same questions, I assume, she'd asked her before, and Sarah gave the same answers she'd given before, and I sat beside her and murmured supportively. The matchmaker promised she'd do her best to find Sarah a good match.

"Shit, I'm really sorry, guys," said the director after she reviewed some of the footage, "but can we do that again? Joel, the label on your soda bottle was showing." The assistant director came over and removed the label from my bottle of Diet Mountain Dew ("If anybody wants us to promote their product, they need to pay for it," he'd said the first day, when I asked him why I had to take my shirt off and replace it with one without a logo), and we shot the entire interview again. Then the director interviewed us each individually. "Sarah has high standards," said the matchmaker in her interview. "She wants to find somebody who she can have as close a relationship with as the one she has with Joel, and it's tricky. But we can do it. It won't be problem."

"Watch this," laughed Sarah. "They'll edit that so she says something like, 'Sarah wants . . . a relationship . . . with Joel . . . it's . . . a problem.'"

Would that she had been wrong.

("We also have a gay division," the matchmaker said to me as we were leaving, handing me her card. "So if you have any friends who might be interested, send them to our website." The URL was nyclubelite.com, and I couldn't imagine that any gay man who saw it wouldn't think it was NYC Lube Lite rather than NY Club Elite. I emailed her to tell her this and suggest she move the site to nycclubelite.com or newyorkclubelite.com; she wrote back, "ha ha ha! you're so funny!" I wanted to reply and tell her no, I meant it, but then I figured I should just leave well enough alone.)

I wasn't thrilled with the idea that America would think I was the type of person to choose a matchmaking company called Club VIP Life, but a few weeks after our visit to the matchmaker's, the crew came over to my house and filmed me discovering the place online, reading very positive reviews, and calling to vet it before bringing Sarah by, so I felt better about the whole thing.

I wish I could say that living your life on camera felt really weird, or, barring that, that living your life on camera started out weird but came to feel really normal, but for me it was more like a game you play at somebody's seriously extended birthday party. I suspect it's different for people on, say, *The Real World* or *Project Runway* or other shows that film their participants twenty-four hours a day, seven days a week, but for *Girls Who Like Boys Who Like Boys*, the crew showed up for several days of filming, went away for a few weeks, came back for several days, went away again, and so forth.

There were four people in the crew: the director, the assistant director (that wasn't actually his title, but it was how I thought of him), the camera guy, and the sound guy. The director was a very petite, very intense woman with very red hair; whenever we took a break or stopped filming for any reason, she could be heard on her cell phone trying to find homes for abandoned puppies. This was very important to her; at one point she failed to place a dog before it was euthanized and it put her out of commission for an hour.

The assistant director was an equally petit Indian guy who looked like he was twelve but wouldn't tell us how old he actually was, and when we Googlestalked him to find out he got really upset. He dressed far more stylishly than anyone I have ever met and appeared to eat nothing and was very funny. Every time they came back into town for filming he would tell me about the men he'd met since the last time they were here, and I would give him dating advice.

The sound guy was really attractive, so although I had figured out fairly quickly how to attach my microphone I preferred to let him stick his hand up my shirt.

The camera guy changed from session to session but rarely said anything at all.

Sarah and I began to refer to our lives, while the crew was there, as taking place on three planets: Planet Earth (where there were no cameras filming our conversations), Planet Reality (on which I pretended to have given her number to somebody I hadn't actually met at a party that I hadn't actually attended because it hadn't actually happened), and Planet Again. Planet Again was by far the most annoying of these, because it took up the most time.

"Guys, can you say that again? The bus ruined the sound when it went by."

"Joel, can you ask her that one more time, but over here? The light was really bad."

"Sarah, can you go back to, 'I don't think you're right,' or whatever you were saying? The radio in the car that passed by was really loud, and we don't have the budget to get the rights for the song."

But the worst part of Planet Again, no question, was the entrances and exits. On the day of the matchmaker scene, for example, once we finished filming the interactions, we went in and out of that building for an hour, and I'm not exaggerating—it really was an *hour*. We took the following shots: our entrance into the building from far away behind us, our entrance into the building from close up behind us, our entrance into the building from in front of the door as we walked up to it, our entrance into the building with the cameraman walking backward in front of us, our entrance into the building from inside the building, our entrance into the elevator from behind us, our entrance into the elevator from inside the elevator, our *exit* from the elevator from inside the elevator, our exit from the elevator from the hall in front of the elevator, our exit from the elevator from in front of the Club VIP Life office door, our entrance into the Club VIP Life office from the far end of the hall, from in front of the office door, from inside the office, our exit from the Club VIP Life office from inside the office, from in front of the office door, from the far end of the hall, our entrance into the elevator from down the hall, in front of the elevator, and inside the elevator, our exit from the elevator from inside the elevator and in front of the elevator, and our exit from the building from inside the building, from the door of the building, with the cameraman walking backward in front of us, and from far away.

And if that was tedious to read, imagine how much worse it was to live.

If I had to evaluate myself and Sarah as citizens of Planet Again, I would say that we were halfway decent. We could usually manage a pretty good recreation of an impromptu exchange we'd just had, or even a more complex scene, complete with surprises and interruptions. There were times, however, when the director asked more of us than we were able to give. The first day she filmed us, for example, a day or two after she'd filmed Mike and me with the waffles, she said, "Can we do the scene where Joel tells you that Mike proposed to him?"

A pause. "But that happened two years ago," I said.

"Yeah, I don't think we can do that convincingly," said Sarah.

"Well, how about we just give it a shot? If it doesn't work, we won't use it."

We went to sit down on the park bench, along with my dogs, Sasha and Zoe (I'd brought them because we figured that if at any point we couldn't think of something to say, we could always just play with the cute animals). We stared at each other in uncomfortable silence as the pigeons cooed around us.

"Those terrible pigeons," Sarah said, which I thought was a good start. "They, like, sit on my windowsill and have babies. They reproduce and shit. The pigeons on my windowsill are getting more action than I am." The scene went on in this fashion until I finally worked my way around to telling Sarah I had news, at which point I held out my hand, making sure the camera caught my engagement ring (the one Mike sized using the One Ring from *The Lord of the Rings*—he had obligingly resized it after the proposal).

"NO!" said Sarah. "That's AMAZING!"

"Yes! Mike proposed! We're going to get married." I gave her what I hoped came across as a smile full of uncontrolled joy.

"Joel, that's *wonderful*! CONGRATULATIONS! I'm so, so happy for you!" She gave me a huge hug.

"Sarah, are you jealous of Joel?" asked the director.

Sarah's brow wrinkled. "Hunh?"

"I mean, you're single and Joel is getting married. Are you jealous?"

"Um . . . no? He has the worst brain chemistry of anybody I know and his boyfriend is obsessed with trees and made him move to Brooklyn?"

"Okay, well, can you talk about how you're happy for him but you really wish you had somebody too?"

"That would be gross."

"Okay, but," said the director, and this went on for another ten minutes, until finally just to make her stop we agreed to attempt an approximation of the exchange she was requesting. I held out my hand again.

"Oh, you've got to be kidding me," said Sarah.

"Nope. Mike proposed. We're going to get married."

"Joel, I am totally happy for you, BUT IT SHOULD BE ME!" She couldn't do it; she had slipped into her let-me-imitate-people-I-want-to-make-fun-of voice. "It's supposed to be me!" Nope, still didn't work.

"Can we not do this anymore, please?" I finally asked the director.

"Sure," she said. "That didn't work. I had to try, but we won't use it."

"No problem," I said.

(They used it. The "it should be me" version. In a scene that led the Salon.com reviewer to call Sarah "a selfish nightmare.")

"Can you guys talk a little bit about why you think gay marriage is important?"

So Sarah fake-asked me to talk to her about some of the legal implications of marriage inequality, and I started talking about the 1,138 federal rights and privileges married people had that we didn't.

"Why do you think the government gives those rights to married people?" she said.

"Well," I said, and I was no longer fake-talking but actually thinking about this, "I guess it's probably because the government has an interest—a reasonable interest—in making marriage attractive. First of all, studies make it pretty clear that married people are healthier, happier, live longer than single people. But even looking at it from a more mercenary point of view, the more people there are who take care of each other, the less the government has to spend to take care of them, right? If I fall down the stairs at age sixty and break something, I'll need help."

"You're going to be spry and fit at sixty," Sarah said loyally.

"Naturally, but in the alternate universe in which I'm not and I fall down, I'll need medical support, I'll need physical support, I'll need emotional support. If Mike has promised to look after me, then he'll probably give me at least some of that support, and help me gain access to some of the rest of it, which means that I won't need to ask the government for all of it."

"Though, since you're an upper-middle-class white man, the government will probably listen when you do ask."

"I wish you were wrong. But I guess married people are given those rights because marriage saves the government a lot of money, while also creating a lot of stability in society."

None of this, of course, made it onto the show. Just the pigeons and the made-up jealousy.

But if getting more people married would further the government's interest, what reason, really, can it have to bar same-sex couples from the state of married bliss?

(It turns out, in fact, that I was wrong; there are plenty of studies suggesting, for example, that single people are happier and healthier than married people, or that, while married men live longer than single men, the numbers are reversed for women. But this is America; the government can't allow its policies to be set by things as silly as data and scientific analysis.)

"So here's my conundrum," I said to Sarah the next time we were being filmed. "I'm getting legally married in Iowa, because I can't do it in New York."

"Right."

"And then I'm having a ceremony somewhere else later on." Much later, in fact, though the reality-show people didn't know yet that they weren't coming anywhere near the thing.

"Right."

"So which one is the real wedding? Like, when do we celebrate our anniversary? And if that's the real one, then why am I having the other one?"

"Whatever, it doesn't matter."

"No, I feel like it's improper to have two weddings. Miss Manners would disapprove." I meant it. I was incredibly uncomfortable; I had to get my wedding right, and this felt wrong. (None of this made it on the show either, which is a shame because I think it's an interesting question and not above the heads of reality-TV viewers.) "This is actually a serious problem."

"So you need to figure out what makes a wedding a wedding."

"Or, put another way, I need to figure out what the definition of marriage is."

"Gays and Lesbians have a right to live as they choose; they don't have a right to redefine marriage for the rest of us." According to the website for the National Organization for Marriage, which is a national organization against marriage, this is the single sentence most effective at persuading people to oppose marriage equality. Over and over again during the last decade or two we've heard arguments about the definition of marriage and redefining marriage and the time-honored definition of marriage and oh my God I want to bash my head in with a dictionary made of granite.

So what *is* the definition of marriage? The whole "between a man and a woman" thing from Proposition 8 doesn't work, because what about all those guys in the Old Testament like Abraham, Isaac, and Jacob? Here, too, Mrs. Grossman's Sunday School instruction has stood me in good stead; a look into the Bible has confirmed my suspicion that they violated the one-man-one-woman principle. Furthermore, in addition to the Big Three we also have King David, who had eight wives and ten concubines, and his son King Solomon, Jesus' twenty-eighth-great grandfather, who must have had some big father issues, because *he* had *three hundred* wives and *seven hundred* concubines (not to mention being the product of a felony—David married Solomon's mother Bathsheba only after he'd had her husband sent to the front lines of battle so he'd be killed and Bathsheba would be single).

In fact, it turns out, the Biblical patriarchs were far from alone in their failure to comply with the one-man-one-woman standard. Here are some more examples of a broader definition than the Defenders of Traditional Marriage would like:

- In seventeenth-century Fukian, China, men could marry men.
- In nations currently governed by Islamic law, a man can marry up to four women (and if he moves to Israel he can stay married to all of them).
- In African tribes like the Nuer of Sudan, women can marry women and even, on occasion, ghosts.
- In Indian tribes like the Nayar of Kerala, a woman can marry as many men as she wants.
- In other Indian tribes like the Toda of Tamil Nadu, when a woman marries a man she also marries all of his brothers.

- In South American tribes like the Caingang, any number of men can marry any number of women.
- In Eskimo societies, couples can marry other couples.
- In Pacific northwestern societies like the Bella Coola and the Kwakiutl, a person can marry another person's foot.
- Jews, according to some, will as of 2040 no longer be subject to the thousand-year Edict of Rabbenu Gershom ordering them to practice monogamy so as not to arouse the hatred of the Christians among whom they lived. (I discovered the others from various sources, especially E. J. Graff's *What Is Marriage For?* and Stephanie Coontz's *Marriage, a History*, but this last I only found out when I tried to crowdsource some question or other about marriage by posting it as my Facebook status and somebody mentioned Rabbenu Gershom in his reply and I went and looked him up, so thank you, Aidan Gilbert, a thousand times thank you, because I think this is *spectacular*.)

Perhaps the simplest way to put it is that the Defenders of Traditional Marriage have a right to live as they choose, but they don't have a right to redefine marriage for the rest of us.

But if marriage isn't "between a man and a woman," then what is it? The English common-law definition (English common law being the starting point for much of American law) is the remarkably similar but more specific "voluntary union for life of one man and one woman, to the exclusion of all others," but that's difficult to take seriously, given the tendency of the conservative married politicians and prelates who espouse it to claim they're hiking in Appalachia while they're actually in Argentina having sex with their mistresses, like former South Carolina Governor Mark Sanford, or to get caught in adulterous affairs with members of their staffs who have appeared in videos with them extolling the virtues of abstinence, like former Senator Mark Souder.

Or with guys in the next bathroom stall, like former Senator Larry Craig, who earned a score of o from the gay-rights group Human Rights Campaign before being arrested for soliciting sex from a male police officer in a St. Paul airport restroom.

Or with guys in their congregations, like Bishop Eddie Long, whose sermons about how same-sexers deserve death culminated in a march he led in support of the Federal Marriage Amendment before he was brought to court for having sex with underage members of a group of his male parishioners known as the Spiritual Sons. "Young man," he apparently told one of them, "you can call me daddy," though it's unclear whether this was before or after the fellatio.

(God, they just make it *too easy*. I almost feel bad for them.)

The one thing that every tradition of marriage seems to have in common, as far as I can tell—even Hammurabi's Code, the four-thousand-year-old codification of the Sumerian Family Laws, which contains decrees like, "If the wife of one man on account of another man has her husband and the other man's wife murdered, both of them shall be impaled" and the surprisingly enlightened "If a man violate the betrothed or child-wife of another man, who has never known a man, and still lives in her father's house, and sleep with her and be surprised, this man shall be put to death, but the wife is blameless"—is that they create kinship.

So I'm going to offer my own sociologically and anthropologically unrigorous definition of marriage as an arrangement whereby, in pledging publicly to take care of each other, previously unrelated people become a family.

This definition has the advantage of including married people among Muslims, the Nuer, the Nayar, the Toda, the Caingang, the Eskimos, the residents of seventeenth-century Fukian, and future Jews, not to mention in Sumeria, Ur (Abraham's homeland), and Las Vegas, thereby rescuing from annulment and sin what I suspect is the greater part of all the marriages ever contracted in the world. It leaves members of the Bella Coola and the Kwakiutl married to other people's feet out in the cold, unfortunately, but

I'm keeping my fingers crossed that they'll forgive me for not being a sociologist.

It also has the further advantage of excluding two bugbears of the Defenders of Traditional Marriage, incest and bestiality. "If we allow gay marriage," they froth rabidly, "what reason can there be not to allow incest? Or bestiality?" Given that I have never heard of or read about a single person who seriously advocates incestuous or interspecies marriage, and neither have you, one would think we could cover same-sexers with the marriage umbrella without losing a whole lot of sleep, but evidently one would be wrong, so my definition should be cause for great relief among the Defenders of Traditional Marriage (I'm sorry for the ironic capitals, but I can't leave them out; no matter how hard I try, my pinky always ends up on the shift key of its own volition, as if somebody had decimated my corpus callosum and left me with Alien Hand Syndrome), since "previously unrelated" rules out incest and "people" rules out puppies and jellyfish, though not, alas, the Real Housewives of New York, New Jersey, Atlanta, Miami, D.C., Beverly Hills, or Orange County.

(The reason not to allow incestuous or bestial marriages, by the way, has nothing to do with same-sexers getting married. If a father wishes to marry his daughter or a farmer his horse, there can be no meaningful consent on the part of the daughter [because of the power imbalance in the family dynamic] or the horse [because it can't understand human speech], and instead of marriage, what you have is rape. *That's* the reason.)

(Another version of this froth is, "What reason can there be not to allow polygamy? Incest? Bestiality?" but it seems ridiculous to put polygamy, which I don't see any problem with, on the same moral level as the others. Changing "people" to "two people" in my definition would take care of this but it would also exclude every marriage in every polygamous society that has ever existed on earth, which seems too costly an exchange.)

When you get married in America today, you promise somebody you'll take care of him or her, and you make that promise in such a way that there's somebody who can hold you to it, even if only in theory. If Mike and I got married in front of a bunch of our friends and family, and in ten years I finally got fed up with his goddamn home and garden shows and said, *that's it, I'm leaving*, there would be a bunch of people in our lives who would say, *but you promised*. This wouldn't necessarily be enough, in the end, to stop us from getting divorced, but according to Robert Cialdini, the author of a book called *Influence: The Psychology of Persuasion*, studies show that giving a commitment to someone in front of other people makes you twice as likely to keep it as giving it to someone with nobody else around.

The people who attend a wedding aren't guests. They're witnesses.

So maybe *that* was how I would manage the question of why I was getting married twice, I thought once I realized this. It was just going to be me, Mike, and the magistrate in Iowa. No witnesses. Which meant that, in a way, an essential part of my definition wouldn't hold true: "publicly." If there were no guests at the Iowa ceremony, then it wouldn't fulfill all the requirements for being a wedding, so there would be a reason to have the second ceremony: without it, we wouldn't be a family.

The more I think about it, the more I think that's what's at the root of all the furor—the idea that same-sexers can forge kinship. After all, if people really didn't think we were capable of committing to caring for those we love, they wouldn't be churning out what Jonathan Rauch calls "Anything But Marriage" laws faster than you can say "Britney Spears and Jason who?," because such laws *do* allow us to make that commitment, albeit in a second-class way. No, it's got to be something about the *word* "marriage."

Because I'll tell you, if the United States government passed a civil-unions law tomorrow and enforced it vigorously, if civilly united same-sex couples really did have every legal right married opposite-sex couples had, it would still be unjust. And here's why:

> Joel and Mike
> Sitting in a tree
> K-I-S-S-I-N-G
> First comes love
> Then comes civil union
> Then comes baby in a baby carriage.

No child is ever going to mock another child in the schoolyard with such a rhyme. It doesn't work that way. No parent is ever going to answer the question, "How do people become a family?" by saying, "Well, when two people love each other very much, they enter a relationship of mutual interdependence and then they have kids."

The word "marriage" means "family."

I think opponents of marriage equality are absolutely terrified of the idea that same-sexers can form families. We can and do form families, of course, but, as long as we can't get married, society can pretend that we don't. That's the reason for all the marriage hysteria. And it's the real reason that we need the right to marry.

There are LGBT activists who oppose the struggle for marriage equality, pointing out that it can distract us from the plight of people whose problems are far more severe than ours, which is true, that it can reinforce societal inequalities, which is true too, that it can stifle the subversion that has always been a part of same-sexer life, which is also true, and that it will benefit only the mostly white and well-to-do subsection of the same-sexer community agitating for the right to marry. But that's where I think they're wrong. I think that marriage equality will benefit the entire same-sexer community, not because of what it will allow married same-sexers to do but because of what it will allow—perhaps force—straight people to perceive. It wasn't lack of a marriage certificate that kept Janice Langbehn from Lisa Pond's side as she died, not the absence of paperwork that led county workers to deliver Harold Scull and Clay Greene's cat to the pound, not a legal question that forced Louise Walpin and Marsha Shapiro to bankrupt themselves caring for their dying son; it was a failure to understand that these were—and that we are—families.

And if my gay marriage, as the overweening subtitle of this book suggests, is going to save the American family, this is how it's going to do it. Every same-sex couple that gets married in this country will create one honest-to-goodness, undeniable American family. And maybe that will be enough to make up for all the marriages—and therefore all the families—being ostensibly destroyed by things like Illinois's civil-union law.

As far as why the Defenders of Traditional Marriage are so horrified at this notion, I'm not sure, but I suspect it's that, if two people of the same sex can become a family, then the family can exist without a man's authority over a woman. And according to Stephanie Coontz, author of *Marriage, a History*, changes in marital gender roles have tended to go hand in hand with changes in societal gender roles; during the Enlightenment, for example, political thinkers began to question absolute monarchy at the same time as ordinary men and women began to choose spouses for themselves rather than simply doing whatever the *paterfamilias* told them to do.

Which means that the idea of same-sexers marrying each other might be the mirror image of a society that can function without the oppression of women.

A frightening vision indeed.

Well, that was a nice try, that oh-it's-not-in-front-of-witnesses-so-it's-not-a-real-wedding thing. It was working pretty well, too, in fact, until my father called and asked whether he could attend the Iowa proceedings. After which my brother called and asked whether *he* could attend the Iowa proceedings. I could hardly say,

"No, you can't come to my wedding or reasonable facsimile thereof," so now we'd have witnesses.

And Mike was *furious*.

"You *promised* me from the beginning that this whole thing would be *low-key*," Mike said to me. "But if your father and brother are coming, then my mother will feel like she has to come, and this is turning into a big deal. You promised me you'd protect me, and you're *breaking your promise*."

Mike was *over* the reality show. He has some control issues (by "some" I mean "a lot of"), and he felt incredibly uncomfortable with the idea that images of him were going to be circulated over which he had no power. I wasn't thrilled with the idea as far as images of myself were concerned, but I guess the *Girls Who Like Boys Who Like Boys* people had persuaded me that it wasn't their plan to mock us like the brides on the first season of *Bridezillas*, who were told only that they were going to be on a series about brides, and if something like that happened then I guessed I'd ruined both our lives, so I was just keeping my fingers really tightly crossed.

(It was perhaps not my wisest move to apprise Mike of my family's plan to attend immediately after we had spent three hours on camera, with Sarah in tow, getting our marriage license application notarized. The notary was a friend of Mike's sister, and once we had filmed her notarizing the application three times ["Are *you* married, Sarah?" she asked during the third take, after the assistant director had come over and whispered in her ear; Sarah rolled her eyes and said, "Jesus *Christ*"] and gone in and out of the building and the office eight hundred times, Mike was clearly relieved to be done with this, until the director was like, okay, let's film the three of you having lunch afterward, which took another two hours.)

"You *know* I hate this," Mike continued, "and yet you have no problem volunteering my time and my energy and my image to be filmed doing whatever they want for however long they want it."

"If you knew how many times they'd asked for you," I said coldly, "and I told them you weren't available, you wouldn't have said that."

"Well, it doesn't feel like that to me. To me it feels like you lied and manipulated me into doing what you wanted me to do and then abandoned me as soon as you could—oh, wait, that's because *you did*."

"Do you think this is easy for me? As of now we're getting married in two weeks, unless we're not, because I don't know if Iowa is a real wedding or not, and you—"

"This is *exactly* what I didn't want! I don't *care* about Iowa! I have *never* cared about Iowa! I don't *care* about the legal and etiquette stuff! I'm doing this for *you* and you're just taking me for granted, and I'm beginning to wonder why we're getting married in the first place."

Neither one of us slept particularly well that night.

"Listen," said Sarah, once the sound guy finished adjusting her microphone, "I may have figured out the solution to your dilemma about which wedding is the real one."

"Really?" My heart lifted. Sarah had wanted to tell me this on the phone, but the director made her wait until we were together so they could film it.

"A wedding in America today is two events. One legal, one ceremonial. They can happen at the same time and place for straight people, but not necessarily for gay people."

"Okay."

"If you and Mike were straight, or you lived in Massachusetts or some other state that allowed same-sex couples to get married, everything would be really simple. You'd invite a bunch of your friends to a ceremony recognizing your commitment to each other, and right after the ceremony you'd sign a piece of paper that meant the government recognized that commitment. It would all feel like one big thing, and the next day you'd wake up and be married."

This made perfect sense, but there was a problem. "Even so," I said, "there's still no reason for us not to go to Connecticut the day before our ceremony and get married there. That would be much more like one event. But by prostituting myself and my wedding for whatever measure of fame might come from this television show on a channel we hadn't even heard of before we auditioned, I've put months and a thousand miles in between the two events. How is that not making it two weddings?"

"Come on, the only thing the extra time and distance do is make the separation easier to see."

None of this conversation made it onto the show, of course. But the more I sat with the idea, the more I thought that maybe this would turn out okay after all. When Mike and I stood in front of the magistrate in Iowa in a week, we'd complete the legal aspect of our wedding but not the ceremonial aspect. That would have to wait. Iowa was my wedding, part one. Part two had yet to be scheduled. And I needed both.

"Sarah, are you sad that Joel's getting married and you're not?"

"Oh, my GOD. I don't know how many times I can tell you that I'm nothing but thrilled that Joel told me he's engaged. Just because he's the one getting married it's not like he's living my fantasy or anything."

(This did make it onto the show, edited as follows: "Joel told me he's engaged. He's living my fantasy. He's the one getting married." As a voice-over to footage of Sarah crying, though what she had actually been crying about in the footage was her terminally ill mother. I wish I were kidding. For what it's worth, this was the edit that made me decide to write this chapter like I'm writing it, so if you were involved in *Girls Who Like Boys Who Like Boys* and you're reading this and you're upset at how much I'm revealing about how the show was made, remember, please, that you talked my ear off about how you were making an honest documentary and then you showed Sarah saying the exact opposite of what she had actually said. It was at this moment, 12:56 to 12:59 in episode 2, that you traded your right to my silence for the chance to make my friend look bad. And if you search your files you'll see that I never signed the nondisclosure agreement, so you can go fuck yourself.)

We hadn't chosen the date on purpose, I explained to the director a couple days before the wedding. It just happened to be the most convenient date. But I was really glad—honored, in fact—to realize what it meant that I was getting married on May 17.

Because May 17, my civil-rights-lawyer father had told me, was the 54th anniversary of the Supreme Court decision in *Brown v. Board of Education*, the case that rang the death knell of segregation in this country (*de jure* segregation, that is; go to any public school in the South and you'll see the shocking health of *de facto* segregation). "Separate is inherently unequal," wrote Chief Justice Earl Warren. What I hadn't realized until my dad explained it to me was that he didn't mean, "If you create black schools and white schools, then, society being what it is, the black schools are going to get less money, lower-quality supplies, and fewer teachers, so for all intents and purposes separate is unequal." It was true that in most cases segregation gave black facilities the short end of the stick, but in *Brown*, the two schools in question were of substantially equal quality. The issue here wasn't the practical effects of segregation; the issue was segregation itself. *That's* what Warren called "inherently unequal." On May 17, 1954, the Supreme Court ruled unanimously not that segregation was wrong because it created an injustice but that segregation was wrong because it *was* an injustice.

(Of course in the early 1990s the Rehnquist Supreme Court vitiated *Brown* so thoroughly it might as well never have happened, with the result that American schools are now more segregated than they've been since 1968. Oh, well: thanks for playing.)

I've already discussed the discomfort I feel agitating for a right demanded by a mostly white, mostly financially comfortable group of people when there are others in America and in the world who are in much worse shape than we are.

This felt, nonetheless, pretty damn meaningful.

Needless to say, none of it found its way into the show.

So finally Mike and I flew to St. Paul, Minnesota, and drove to nearby Rochester to stay with Mike's cousin DJ and DJ's boyfriend, Kevin. Mike still wasn't happy about what we were doing, but having expressed his anger he was much better able to weather his own displeasure. After leaving our bags at DJ's house, we went to the mall and visited Kevin at the Zales Jewelry store he managed. (The Zales was apparently not doing an extraordinary amount of business, probably because it was one of six jewelry stores *in the same mall.* This made me think that either a) somebody had a really bad sense of retail design or b) Minnesotans were a lot richer than we realized.)

The next day, after the assistant director's repeated phone calls, Mike's acquiescence to the request for nice clothes, and our five-hour drive to Cedar Rapids (our first stop was the county registrar's office, where we managed to pick up our marriage license with only one small hitch, when Mike threatened to murder me if, as it appeared, I had actually left my photo ID in Minnesota, but it turned out I had only been looking in the wrong pocket of my bag), we headed over to the magistrate's office on Planet Again, where we drove into and out of the parking lot several times, and finally walked with my father, my brother, Mike's mother, Kevin, DJ, and a camera crew into the magistrate's waiting room.

"Look over this and let me know if you want to make any changes in what I'm going to say," said the magistrate, obviously nervous in front of the camera, as he handed me a copy of the ceremony text.

I glanced at it briefly and asked, "Can you add 'according to the law' here or something like that?"

"Um . . . why?"

I opened my mouth and let about thirty seconds of my the-only-way-I-can-do-this-and-not-feel-like-I'm-getting-married-twice-when-I-get-married-again-later-on-is-to-treat-this-as-the-legal-half-of-something-that-has-another-ceremonial-half thing escape before I shut it again, hoping to God that they wouldn't show this part. (They didn't. One of the few editorial choices for which I am grateful.)

The magistrate seemed sympathetic to my concern but, in the end, not sympathetic enough to change anything. "Well, if I'm marrying you," he said gently, "then . . . it means you're married. That's what the law says."

I opened the door—oh, hey, it's Sarah, remember to look SURPRISED!—and we got set up, after which the magistrate told Mike and me to hold hands and repeat, "I take you to be my spouse, to have and to hold, from this day forward, to love, honor, and cherish, to comfort and respect, in sorrow and in joy, as long as we both shall live." Then, once we were finished, he said, "And now, forasmuch as you have made your vows, each to the other, I pronounce you are married," and we kissed.

Then we signed our marriage certificate—"Oh, you have to use blue or black ink," said the magistrate, and offered me a Bic to replace the purple fountain pen I'd taken out of my pocket to sign my name—Mike's mother and Sarah witnessed it, and we were done. Then, to celebrate, we had lunch at the only restaurant in Cedar Rapids still standing from Mike's childhood, a Greek place, where the waitress claimed to remember him from thirty-five years ago and where the camera crew, on break, was very impressed by the flaming cheese we ordered. After that we went to Dairy Queen, where I'd never been and where I instantly wanted to spend the rest of my life. The director didn't make anybody do anything over again, possibly because there were regular people involved rather than people who had auditioned to be on a reality show, so the whole thing felt much more natural, though my brother's friends still mock him for the toast he was filmed giving over our ice cream. Finally, when we were done, the director made Sarah stand there as everybody else left so that they could get a fake poignant shot of her being sad and alone, neither of which she was.

I think the show actually had good intentions, but when it aired, despite all the footage they had of me and Sarah being very funny in ways that made complex issues seem pretty straightforward, mostly they just used shots in which I stammered a lot. To be sure, I *do* stammer a lot, so that couldn't have been difficult for them, but I don't know that it made for particularly compelling TV, and I think they could have dug deeper without losing the audience. Toward the end of the season, in fact, they began to, and the show became more interesting, but for me it was too little, too late.

On principle I'm opposed to reality TV, because every show on the air that creates characters from footage of real people takes a job away from a writer. That's precisely the reason that there are so many reality shows: when the Writers Guild of America went on strike in 2007, the TV networks had to have *something* to program, and reality TV fit the bill, with, among others, *Make Me a Supermodel*, *The Celebrity Apprentice*, *How To Look Good Naked*, *American Gladiators*, *Dance War: Bruno vs. Carrie Ann*, *Ghost Hunters International*, *Celebrity Rehab with Dr. Drew*, *Scott Baio is 46 . . . and Pregnant*, *My Fair Brady . . . Maybe Baby?*, *The Moment of Truth*, *Miss America: Reality Check*, and *Gone Country*. The problem is that by the time the strike was over, TV executives had realized how much they could accomplish without writers, and now we have Honey Boo-Boo.

The weird thing is that I still buy reality TV completely when I watch it. Even though I know how fake these things are—because I have to assume that most of the shows I watch are a hell of a lot faker than *Girls Who Like Boys Who Like Boys*—I still totally believe the villain as the villain, totally gasp that So-and-so said such-and-such, totally commit emotionally to it all. Knowing how artificial it is doesn't make me any less susceptible to the editing.

A few days after the Iowa wedding, I had an answer to the question of why I was getting married twice.

It was because after the first time I didn't feel married.

At all.

Though at the time the state of New York didn't grant marriage licenses to same-sex couples, it did recognize such marriages performed in other states, which meant that my home state considered me married. I could go on Mike's insurance when it had open enrollment in November, which I fully intended to do, if only because his doctor, who didn't take my insurance, had a waiting room with décor so soothing it made me feel at one with the universe. But in conversation with friends, when I referred to Mike as my husband, a small part of me felt like a fraud—like, let me perform a little casuistry for you and I'll show you how it's so. I had had a marriage ceremony but not a wedding. Or I had had a wedding but not a marriage. Or something like that.

So I guessed there were two options.

Either I'd feel married after the actual wedding ceremony, when I said "I do" (or whatever I ended up saying) in front of my friends and family and no TV cameras.

Or I wouldn't feel married until legal marriage equality covered all of America, the fifty states and the federal government. In which case it might be a while.

Except a third, disturbing possibility occurred to me as well.

In *Antigone*, written around 442 B.C., after his nephew Polyneices dies in an attack on the city, King Creon of Thebes orders that Polyneices' corpse be left out, unburied, to be eaten by birds, so that his soul will never reach the underworld. Creon's niece Antigone buries her brother anyway; when Creon asks her why she defied his edict, she says, "Zeus didn't announce it to me, and Justice didn't ordain laws like it. And I didn't think your decree was strong enough to override the unwritten, unfailing laws of the gods; those laws are not for today or yesterday but forever, and no one knows when they were made."

Antigone won first prize in the festival in which it was performed, but if Sophocles had written it today, I suspect that, given the current political climate, he would have had a difficult time staging it. Because this was the first time in the history of the world that anybody had said anything like this, the first time anybody had ever been so brazen as to claim a right not granted by the state. This was the birth of the idea of moral law, without which no modern discussion of civil rights could take place.

I had, I believed, the moral right to marry Mike, but I didn't have the legal right to do so. Newt Gingrich did not have the moral right, having started a shouting match with his first wife in front of their children, in the hospital room where she was recovering from cancer surgery, about the terms of the divorce he wanted so he could marry the woman he had been cheating on her with for a year (whom he later divorced so he could marry the woman he had been cheating on *her* with for a year), to campaign for president as a protector of the family, but he had the legal right to do so. And when your moral rights and your legal rights don't coincide, it *fucks you up*.

What if the thirty-seven years I'd spent as a person without the legal right to be married had misshapen me, like a carefully trained and tortured bonsai tree, not to occupy a space in which I could understand emotionally that I now had that right?

I thought about the black Americans who were slaves on New Year's Eve of 1863 and who the next day, when the Emancipation Proclamation went into effect, were free. They had spent their lives with their moral right to be free and their legal right to be free in misalignment. Once those rights came together, was there some emotional space those free men and women couldn't occupy? Was there a part of some of them that couldn't fit into a world in which they were free?

I thought about Judith Simon, the first girl ever to have a bat mitzvah (the Jewish rite of passage into adulthood, reserved until 1923 for men). Until that moment, she had spent her life with her moral right to be recognized as an adult and her legal right to be recognized as an adult out of joint. Once those rights aligned themselves, was she able to think of herself officially as a Jewish adult? If not, what then?

What if I *never* felt married?

The answer lay, I came to realize, in the same-sexers who would be born the day after marriage equality was the law of the land in the United States, because they would be the ones who would never know an America in which they couldn't marry the people they loved, just like black people born on January 1, 1864, would never know an America in which they were slaves—they wouldn't have any trouble occupying that emotional space blocked to me.

So perhaps it didn't matter too much if I never felt married, because they would.

6

Planning the Ceremony

W e need to have a conversation about planning the ceremony," I said to Mike one Saturday afternoon about a month after we'd returned from Iowa.

"You keep saying that," he said, "but then you never actually start a conversation about planning the ceremony." This was not an animadversion I could duck, because it was true; I never actually started a conversation about planning the ceremony.

"But that's because before now we haven't had enough books about planning ceremonies to make sure we did it right." Things had gotten complicated enough, I felt, that Karen Bussen's *Simple Stunning Wedding Organizer* was no longer enough on its own to guide me.

"And what's different now?"

"While you were at the hardware store the guy came with my Amazon delivery."

"Didn't I forbid you to buy any more books?"

"Yes, but I didn't listen." I grabbed his hand and dragged him into the kitchen, where piles and piles of new wedding-planning books teetered dangerously on the counter.

"Okay, you definitely cannot buy any more books."

"Whatever you say, honey." We sat down and I grabbed a book at random and opened it. "You've got the ring and the man of your dreams," I read, "and now it's time to start planning the wedding—although if you're like most women, you've been planning your wedding since you were a little girl. From the gorgeous gown and cascades of flowers to the perfect reception at the perfect location, you've envisioned your special day, right down to the very last detail." I looked up at him. "See, that's the problem."

"What, that you're not like most women?"

"Ha ha sort of," I said. "I haven't been planning my wedding since I was little. I never thought of marriage as part of my possible future. So I have no idea what I want to do for the ceremony. That's why I've been avoiding trying to figure it out."

And I meant it. The fantasies I had begun to entertain during puberty of the tall, well-muscled blond with whom I would fall in love at first sight, who would reciprocate that love, who would complete me, who would have me at hello, who would bear a striking resemblance to my computer science teacher, Mr. Russell— these fantasies had not included marriage, not in any serious way. Neither had the fantasies of the beefy brunet who had all the aforementioned virtues except he would bear a striking resemblance to David Hasselhoff (shut up, he was hot in the eighties).

Early in my junior year of college, one of my straight female friends called me to tell me she'd been dumped by her boyfriend of five years. Of course I ran over to her dorm room so we could glut ourselves with ice cream and cookies, and as we ate she talked about her ruined wedding fantasies. She would never have the dress that made her look fifteen pounds lighter, never have the organ playing the *St. Anne Prelude and Fugue* as she floated down the aisle, never assemble the bridal party in uncomfortable tuxedoes and impeccably tailored dresses that made all her bridesmaids look slightly less attractive than she did. I listened sympathetically and at appropriate moments spit vile imprecations at the reprobate who had thrown her over, because I am a good friend and because to pass up an opportunity to glut myself with ice cream and cookies would be foolish, but, although I knew far too well the pain of being dumped, there was a very real way in which I just didn't get any of the wedding-of-my-dreams stuff. These were ideas to which I had never assigned any emotional weight, because any such assignment would have been a waste of energy; it couldn't end in anything but disappointment. So while I understood my friend's pain, its source was a black box, enigmatic and impenetrable.

And now, as an adult, I had spent the last seven years in confusion about when Mike and I ought to celebrate our anniversary. Our first date? That would be February 11. Our first date a year later the second time around, after, having dumped him, I came to my senses and asked him out again and he was fool enough to say yes? That would be November 9. The day I told him I loved him? That depends whether you count the first time, when I followed it immediately with "more than the Internet" (October 6), or the time I said it without qualification (God only knows; this was obviously far too momentous an occasion for me to remember its date). If we had been a married heterosexual couple, it would have been easy: we'd celebrate our anniversary on the date of our wedding. But as same-sexers, try as we might, we hadn't been able to jury-rig an acceptable substitute. (If we'd been an unmarried heterosexual couple we might still have been in the same discomfiting position, but it would be by our choice, and if we got sick of confusion there would have been a quick remedy.)

So how could I know what I wanted out of a wedding if marriage equality was something that for most of my life I'd thought of—if I'd thought of it at all—in the same way I'd thought of the Easter Bunny or the spine of the Democratic Party: something that people have fun talking about but that doesn't actually exist? How was I to decide whether I wanted a small, tasteful wedding in a quiet hall somewhere or a lavish spectacle in the Parthenon?

"Well, okay," said Mike. "What *do* we know?"

"We know that we're wearing morning clothes."

We knew that we were wearing morning clothes—that is, tails, waistcoat, and maybe even top hat—because I wanted my wedding to be as formal as possible. (Tuxedos with black tie were originally what one wore for occasions on which *informal* dress was called for, and tuxedos with white tie and tails for more formal occasions, though irrespective of the color of the tie tuxedos were only for the evening—it would have been the height of gaucherie to wear a tuxedo of any sort during the daytime. But the world has moved on since then, and if we no longer give babies laudanum to make them stop crying and go to sleep then I suppose fashion too must keep pace with the times.) I intended to avoid any and all innovations, personalizations, and cute touches. My wedding would be devoid of whimsy.

"I don't get it," Mike had said when I first explained this to him. "Why is it so important to you to wear morning clothes?"

I couldn't answer him for the life of me, so I distracted him by accidentally on purpose spilling strawberry jam on his shirt; once I removed it—the shirt, that is, not the jam—the afternoon proceeded as one might expect.

But I've thought about it a lot in the years since this conversation, and I believe there are a few reasons it mattered so much to me. First of all, as an ardent devoté of Miss Manners, I believe with her that there is a "difference between making an occasion enjoyable and making a significant event into a mockery." I once went to a commitment ceremony where the two grooms exchanged butt plugs instead of rings. And I had a great time, as did everybody else, but if I was demanding the right to participate in a ritual that would transform me in the eyes of the society I lived in, and then when I won it I made fun of it, then as far as I was concerned I was either a hypocrite (oh, I never thought it was actually that important) or a morass of self-loathing (I don't deserve the real thing, so I'm going to adulterate it). Of course I *am* a hypocrite and a morass of self-loathing, but I saw no reason to make those character traits public.

Or maybe it would be better to think in philosopher Walter Kaufmann's terms. "The absence of all ritual," he writes in *Faith of a Heretic*, "would entail nearly total blindness to the mysteries of this world, while ritual provides occasions when one regularly tries to listen for the voice that the rest of the time one is prone to forget." How would I be able to hear that voice if I was busy working my vows as stand-up comedy? How could I attend to any mystery if I was worried about whether my dog the ring-bearer would be able to trot down the aisle without stopping to poop?

Comedy is the other side of tragedy; neither can exist without the other. And if there was one moment to protect from the intrusion of tragedy—and therefore from the intrusion of comedy—it was the instant in which I became one with my fiancé. If anything was sacred in the world, then I wanted that moment to be sacred. And humans are slow creatures, so before we arrived at that moment we would need a while to calm down and stop giggling and make room for what might allow us, in however clumsy and clay-footed a way, to transcend ourselves.

That was why we were wearing morning clothes at my wedding.

And as I think about it now, there was another reason, too, one that has to do with the infantilization of same-sexers I've discussed. If marriage equality is in some ways about the right to be held to just as high a standard as straight people, then I wanted to set that standard as high as I possibly could and to celebrate its Olympian loftiness. By refusing to accede to any dilutions of the ritual, I could show my refusal to accede to any dilutions of the responsibility I was asking to assume.

"We also know," I said, straightening one of the piles of wedding-planning books that seemed on the verge of collapse, "that we're getting married outside."

When we first started talking about a wedding, years before the actual proposal, I told Mike that my dream location was St. Mark's Basilica in Venice, but I acknowledged that the Catholic Church was unlikely to be brought to its senses while I was still of marriageable age. My worries about the degree of resistance of the

Catholic Church took a back seat, however, when Mike told me about *his* dream wedding, for which we wore shorts and T-shirts. As to a location, when I mentioned St. Mark's he laughed condescendingly and said, "No, silly. We're going to go to a forest upstate and get married in a clearing."

I was dismayed. I hate nature; as far as I'm concerned, if you are overwhelmed by a compulsion to look at trees, the Internet provides innumerable opportunities, and if that's not enough you can buy a calendar. I had long since learned, however, that one of Mike's many flaws was a weakness for things that photosynthesize, and I knew from painful experience that an argument from emotion would hold little weight with him. In my mental flailing I finally decided that the practical route was the way to go: raise enough logistical objections, reasonably enough, and he would be forced to abandon his lunacy. "But where will the food be for the reception?" I said calmly.

"It'll be off to the side, on tables. We'll eat buffet-style."

"And where will our guests sit?" I asked.

"People will just stand in a circle."

"No one is *standing in a circle* at my wedding." I felt desperation beginning to mount and had to work hard to keep it out of my voice. "If we're getting married outdoors, we're bringing chairs for the guests."

"Oh, come on. They can sit if you want them to, but we don't have to bring chairs."

"Really? Then where will they sit?" It was very difficult by now to keep from shrieking.

"On the beautiful green earth."

I'm not making this up. He actually said "on the beautiful green earth." And he sort of meant it, too. He was teasing me, but he actually would have been happy with a wedding at which everybody sat on the ground. It drove me crazy. Who thinks a wedding is about stupid crap like community and togetherness and love?

After excruciating hours of back and forth we were eventually able to find a compromise: I said I would be willing to get married outside if he was willing to wear morning clothes. This would give the event the solemnity without which I couldn't participate, while at the same time fulfilling Mike's inexplicable desire to involve dirt. Relieved thus to have averted catastrophe, I said, "Okay, next question: what kind of invitations are we going to send?"

"Oh, we won't," he said.

"Then how," I said nervously, "will our friends know about the wedding?"

"We'll just tell them."

"It's at moments like this that I really wish I drank."

"If you want, we can send out an Evite."

"I rue the day I laid eyes on you."

"Me, too, honey."

In the end, the list Mike and I came up with that day in the kitchen, following the instructions of my new library of wedding-planning books, looked like this:

Wedding To-Do List

1. Decide location.
2. Decide date.
3. Draw up guest list.
4. Register for gifts.
5. Plan ceremony.
6. Plan party.
7. Plan honeymoon.

Conversations about morning clothes and forests were all very well and good when the wedding was simply a matter of theory; now that theory was heading toward practice, however, I thought, girding my loins in preparation for the battle that choosing the right outdoor venue for the ceremony would involve, the story might be different. And then Mike said, "Why don't we have the wedding outside at the Brooklyn Botanic Garden?" and I said, "Sure, why not?" and that was that.

My lack of imaginative history when it came to weddings gave me an advantage, it was turning out; all I knew was that we were having our wedding in an outdoor grand location, but beyond that I had no specifics in mind, so the first outdoor grand location Mike came up with, a garden world-famous for its miles and miles of beautifully cultivated flowers, was absolutely fine by me. Shocked at the lack of further conflict, I ungirded my loins, but I decided to keep the greaves nearby, in case not all our decisions would be made this easily.

According to the Brooklyn Botanic Garden's website, chairs were not allowed at ceremonies conducted outside. Since as I've already made clear I had no intention of allowing my wedding guests to sit on the earth, its beauty and/or greenness notwithstanding, they would have to stand, which necessity would have the salutary effect, I realized, of making the wedding very, very short—fifteen minutes, twenty tops, and then back to our house for the party.

The Brooklyn Botanic Garden's website went on to explain that wedding ceremonies on its grounds were held at 9:00 a.m., which I was willing to accept even though I thought it was an un- civilized hour because it meant that afterward we could serve people champagne and cake rather than much more expensive hard liquor and actual food, and limited to sixty guests, which answered for me the question of small and tasteful vs. lavish spectacle. I was uncomfortable doing things in this manner, because I felt one ought to draw up the guest list first and then find a venue that would fit everybody rather than the other way around, but once again my wedding-fantasy-less upbringing stymied me, because I'd never thought about who I wanted to invite in the first place.

So, improperly prioritized as it might have been, I decided to cling to the Brooklyn Botanic Garden, because it was one of the only measures of stability I'd found so far.

The decision about the date proved unexpectedly easy to make when, looking over the list of when the Garden was available we found the striking option of 10/10/10. The insufferable cuteness was not a thing we could resist, so we had a wedding date, as well as a guarantee that neither one of us would ever forget our anniversary.

"That date is good," I said, "because it's on a Sunday, and Jewish weddings are never on Saturday."

"We're having a Jewish wedding?"

"Oh, my God! Something else I knew I wanted for the wedding! And I didn't even realize I'd known it! Except, crap, honey, we need to discuss this. What kind of wedding do *you* think we should have?"

"Sure, a Jewish wedding is fine, whatever you want."

I looked at him. "What do you mean, 'Sure, a Jewish wedding is fine, whatever you want'?"

"Look, don't turn into Groomzilla. It just doesn't really matter to me."

So we sat down to make a sixty-person guest list, which dropped to thirty once we'd taken care of family. This made things tricky, because if we limited the list to truly, deeply close friends, there would probably be ten, and if we expanded it to just plain good friends, there would be a hundred. Finally, though, after several evenings of complicated chart-making, we had what seemed a good collection of people.

Wedding To-Do List

1. ~~Decide location.~~
2. ~~Decide date.~~
3. ~~Draw up guest list.~~
4. Register for gifts.
5. Plan ceremony.
6. Plan party.
7. Plan honeymoon.

For a man who hasn't been to synagogue since 2002, when I went to New York's gay synagogue one Friday night to meet men and was horrified to find everybody actually paying attention to the liturgy instead of cruising, I am surprised sometimes by the ferocity with which I identify as Jewish. It can't spring from any kind of relationship with God, since I am as certain that there is no God as I am that I am a biped, and if I believed there *were* a God I would bend all my will to seeing Him prosecuted for what He'd done to the world. My sense of Jewish identity can't be founded on an idea of community, since when I'm around too many Jews for too long I find myself getting angry in the same way I do around too many white gay men, only the question in this case is some variant of HillaryorObamawho'sbetterfortheJews. I suppose my vigor could stem from pride in being part of a group associated with valuing knowledge and inquiry, but somehow that seems a little weak.

What I do know is that, for me, one of the most important aspects of being Jewish is being *not Christian*—in other words, being part of a minority. I'm not planning on having children, since I hate and fear them, but I've always said that if I did by some unfortunate chance come into possession of a child I would insist on raising it Jewish so that it knew what being an outsider felt like. This would be a way, as I see it, of guaranteeing a sense of compassion.

Given this awareness unaccompanied by a corresponding conscious understanding, I suspected that before I planned a wedding ceremony I ought to find out more about what the whole thing meant. I knew you needed a chuppah (wedding canopy) and you stomped on a glass at the end, but other than that I was a blank slate.

"Who should officiate?" I asked Mike.

"Whoever you want," he said.

"How about Rabbi Rachel?"

"Ooh, I like her."

I called Rachel and left her a message asking her whether she could perform our ceremony, oh and by the way what the hell did we need in our ceremony?

Wedding To-Do List

1. ~~Decide location.~~
2. ~~Decide date.~~
3. ~~Draw up guest list.~~
4. Register for gifts.
5. Plan ceremony.   PROGRESS
6. Plan party.
7. Plan honeymoon.

"We have everything we need as far as material possessions," I said to Mike.

"Well, our own private island."

"Or Karl Rove's head on a platter."

"I don't think anybody we're inviting could afford that."

"So I think we should have our guests contribute to charity instead," I offered.

"That's a nice idea."

"The problem is that we're not allowed to tell them this."

"Hunh?"

It's true. If anybody asks, you're allowed to say, oh, really, we don't want anything, we'd prefer to share our happiness with others less fortunate, can you make a donation to your favorite charity in our honor instead? But if they don't ask, you're not allowed to say, "Oh, by the way, if you're thinking of buying us a wedding gift, we'd prefer that you make a donation to charity," because then you're letting people know you expect them to buy you a gift, which is rude.

I thought for a few days about this and finally remembered the scheme my friend Julia came up with when she was planning her wedding some years ago and found herself face to face with the same problem, so I chose, as has often been the case, to take advantage of my friend's cleverness. I would have one of our guests email all the other guests saying he or she suspected that instead of gifts what we really wanted was donations to charity.

Though I also decided to keep my eye out for any store that offered Karl Rove's head for sale, in which case I would change my mind at once.

Wedding To-Do List

1. ~~Decide location.~~
2. ~~Decide date.~~
3. ~~Draw up guest list.~~
4. ~~Register for gifts.~~
5. Plan ceremony.   PROGRESS
6. Plan party.
7. Plan honeymoon.

A Jewish wedding, Rachel explained when she called to say yes, is a fairly straightforward affair. Not even the glass-stomping is required. The only part that's absolutely necessary is the signing of the ketubah—more or less a pre-nup that makes the wedding official. But there are also a number of other traditions commonly included, of which the chuppah and the glass-stomping are two:

The reason the ceremony is usually held under a chuppah is to symbolize that the whole thing is taking place in the house of the Big Guy upstairs. I asked my friend Michelle, whose wedding took place under the most gorgeous chuppah I've ever seen—her mother had commissioned it for the occasion—whether we could borrow it, and she said she'd be thrilled.

One decision made.

The bride often circles the groom either three or seven times. Three symbolizes the three virtues of marriage (righteousness, justice, and lovingkindness); seven is the Biblical number of perfection—God built the world in seven days, so you were building your own world for the two of you, though it was unclear to me why the woman had to do all the work. As far as the number, I liked the extravagance of seven but I worried about getting dizzy. Rachel suggested that each of us do three circles around the other and then one together in opposite directions, which I couldn't really picture, because I have a bad sense of spatial dynamics, but I trusted her.

The bride's face is often completely covered with a veil, which the groom lifts before signing the ketubah. This is because Jacob the Biblical patriarch, after he had worked for Rebecca's father Laban for seven years, didn't check to make sure it was Rebecca he was marrying; he paid a great deal for this lack of foresight, because sneaky Laban made a last-minute switch with his older daughter, Leah, and it was her that Jacob actually married, which meant that, in order to marry Rachel, Jacob had to put in another seven years working for Laban. The unveiling was ultimately worked into the standard wedding ceremony to protect grooms from the treachery of their wily fathers-in-law.

I did not wish to wear a veil.

My wily, treacherous father's vision was so bad, furthermore, that, if he tried to fool Mike by substituting my brother for me, he would have no idea whether or not he'd succeeded, or probably whether he'd even started with me in the first place, so there was really no point.

The groom usually gives the bride a ring and says, "Behold, you are consecrated to me with this ring according to the law of Moses and Israel." Mike was not Jewish, however, despite being something of a matzah queen, and had therefore no cause to do anything according to the law of Moses and Israel.

On the to-think-about list.

The last thing that happens under the chuppah is a set of seven blessings, pronounced sometimes by the person performing the ceremony, sometimes by seven different wedding guests. So we had to figure out whether these should be in English or Hebrew, or whether in fact we should have them at all.

This was a little overwhelming, especially since all Mike would say whenever I asked him about any of it was that he was fine with whatever I decided.

Wedding To-Do List

1. ~~Decide location.~~
2. ~~Decide date.~~
3. ~~Draw up guest list.~~
4. ~~Register for gifts.~~
5. Plan ceremony.   ~~PROGRESS~~   MORE PROGRESS
6. Get ketubah.
7. Plan party.
8. Plan honeymoon.

Mike and I have mutually exclusive vacation styles: he likes to walk around and see sights, while I like to stay in the hotel room and read and sleep and watch TV. (I don't know whether this is a Jewish thing or a my-family thing. But my brother, the last time somebody invited him to go camping, said, "Camping was what people did before we had air conditioning and cable," and I'm with him 100 percent.) There was, however, an obvious compromise: a Caribbean cruise would allow Mike to do the former and me to do the latter, with a little flexibility in case either one of us wanted to break character.

As I sent Mike email after email about various cruises I found online, however, trying to determine which one would be the best choice, his replies got both fewer and more annoyed.

"Look," he finally wrote. "I don't care. You just decide."

Okay, I thought. *But this is starting to feel weird.*

Wedding To-Do List		
1. ~~Decide location.~~		
2. ~~Decide date.~~		
3. ~~Draw up guest list.~~		
4. ~~Register for gifts.~~		
5. Plan ceremony.	~~PROGRESS~~	MORE PROGRESS
6. Get ketubah.		
7. Plan party.		
8. Plan honeymoon.	PROGRESS?	

It was when I started looking for a ketubah, the one absolute requirement of a Jewish wedding, that things started to fall apart.

A disappointing majority of the ketubahs I saw online were really unattractive. They were all in dull or dark browns or reds or blues, and the backgrounds were almost universally Sean Cody beige, which I thought was inappropriate for a document that purported to bind me to a man with a last name. (Sean Cody, for those of you who don't know, runs a website featuring muscular young men identified only by monikers like "Dakota" and "Bryce" having sex with each other in rooms so drably painted and cheerlessly appointed that they make the activity one engages in while watching them so dreary it's almost impossible to complete.)

I found a few websites that had absolutely gorgeous ketubahs, but the problem here was that I knew Mike would hate the ones I loved because they were too whimsical or too extravagant or too purple. At one point I thought we'd finally found the answer, because I showed Mike a very attractive blue ketubah from ketubahworks.com and he said, "Oh, that's really nice!" in a tone of voice that made it sound like he really meant it, so I figured the search was over, but then a couple weeks later I told somebody on the phone that we'd picked a ketubah and after I hung up Mike was like, "What do you mean, we've picked a ketubah?" and I showed him the one he'd said was really nice and he said, "I've never seen that before and I hate it." No matter how vehemently I insisted to him that he'd said differently before, he refused to believe me. It was just like when he'd denied saying he was too busy to do couples therapy and our failure to continue was actually my fault. I wondered whether I ought to be worried about early-onset Alzheimer's.

But one Thursday I finally found a ketubah website that I liked (mpartworks.com/ketubah_studio.htm) and that I thought he might like too. "The ketubahs on here are gorgeous," I wrote in an email I sent to him along with the URL. "Are there any that you particularly like?"

Three days later, he still hadn't responded. Finally on Sunday night over dinner I said, "So have you looked at the ketubahs on the website I emailed you?"

"No," he said. "I haven't had time. I've been really busy at work." *Not this weekend, you haven't,* I thought. "I'll look at them soon, I promise."

When I asked again on Wednesday, he said, "Would you stop badgering me about it? I'll get to it."

"When?"

"When I get to it."

"*Fine.* We'll do what you want and just leave it until the last minute and—"

"What I *want*," said Mike, "is to be involved in the process of planning this wedding without having to discuss every single detail of every single decision with you for an hour."

"It might help if you ever bothered to tell me a single thing about what you have in mind."

"Fine. I'll look at them later tonight."

He didn't.

"Why," he said when he got home the next day, tense, "is there a message from a caterer on our voicemail confirming a meeting with you tomorrow?"

"Oh, I called Cathy's friend Marcus to talk to him about catering the party."

Irritation flooded his voice. "And you were going to tell me this when?"

"What? I figured you'd want me to take care of it."

"Oh, my God. Can you not tell the difference between things that are important and things that aren't?"

"That's it," I said. "We're going to couples therapy."

7

Taking Stock of the Relationship

S o," said Dr. Basescu during our first meeting, "what brought you two in to see me today?"

"Well, the short version," I said, "is that I made Mike go on a reality show and now he's deeply resentful but we're getting married in two months and we've wanted to do couples therapy for a while anyway and his individual therapist said you were terrific and gave him your number."

"And the long version?"

"That," said Mike, "is a little more complicated."

I have been online for an hour looking at pictures of my wonderful, handsome, dashing, brilliant, charming husband and thinking about how wonderful, handsome, dashing, brilliant, and charming he is.

Not my husband Mike, but my new husband, Cole. I'm sure Mike will understand, though; he's a reasonable man, and I'm almost positive I'll give him the ring back, so he won't be out all that much.

Cole is my new husband because I saw him in a reading of a musical last week (he's an actor) and friended him on Facebook along with a message telling him how daring and generous I thought his performance had been, and then I saw him in a reading of another piece again yesterday (it's final project season at the musical theater writing program where I teach) and ran into him before-hand; he thanked me for my message and apologized for not writing back and I told him it was no problem and then he started asking me about myself and all I wanted to do was gaze deep into his eyes and reveal my soul to him but I was in the middle of helping some student with a problem or something—that's the trouble with students; they always want you to take the time to *teach* them things—so I told him we'd talk afterward, but then when I came up to him afterward he was looking in another direction and couldn't see me and I was too scared to try and get his attention because what if actually he didn't really like me after all and if I just avoided him then he could never break my heart by rejecting me so I ducked into the men's room and washed my hands for five minutes thinking about what I would cook when he introduced me to his parents and then I came out and he was gone.

(This is an indication, by the way, of how much better medicated I am than I used to be. If this had happened in my early thirties, I would still have ducked into the men's room, but instead of spending those five minutes washing my hands I would have spent them crying.)

I loved couples therapy. Part of the reason for this was that, rather than being an exploration of what we'd both unwittingly been doing to make the relationship more difficult and a journey to discover what each of us could do to bring the other closer, for the first month and a half it consisted of the therapist telling Mike how he was wrong.

(I am perfectly willing to admit that this was my subjective experience and that in fact our couples therapist may simply have been a brilliant tactician who actually spent a month and a half telling *me* how *I* was wrong and making me believe she was doing the opposite.)

"Mike, do you hear what Joel is saying about what he needs from you as far as participation in the wedding planning?" she would say, but she never asked me whether I heard what he was saying, because it was obvious that *I did.*

"Mike, can you see how Joel might get frustrated when you use language like 'just take care of the little stuff with the ceremony and check with me about the important things'?"

"Mike, would you be willing to have the sort of conversation Joel is asking for about the ketubah?"

The best part about all of this was that she had been recommended by Mike's individual therapist, so if he didn't like it there was absolutely nothing he could say.

According to Mike's friend Tony, every couple has one problem. Every time they get into a fight, every time they start calling each other names or wishing secretly or openly for a cliff to push each other off, it always boils down in the end to an expression of that problem. This makes a lot of sense to me, as whenever Mike and I get into a fight, it always boils down in the end to an expression of the problem that he is an asshole.

One Saturday a few years ago, for example, we went to the movies. I take full responsibility for the fact that we were late, as I was dawdling when I ought to have been getting ready to go. We got to the theater just in time to catch the beginning of the movie, we thought, but once we had our popcorn and Peanut Butter M&Ms (for me) and nachos and cheese (for Mike), we realized we hadn't taken into consideration the fact that this theater had eight floors and escalators that moved at the speed of evolution; when we reached our screen on the top floor, therefore, the movie—not the previews but the actual movie—had already started, so I said we couldn't go in.

Mike exploded. He sat on a bench in the lobby, his rapidly cooling nachos perched precipitously on his knees, and yelled at me for half an hour (by which I mean he spoke sharply to me for like four minutes). I knew it drove him crazy to be late, he said, and if I'd made us late then I had no right to say we couldn't see the movie once it had begun, and he was sick and tired of my never considering his feelings, and didn't I realize that he needed taking care of every once in a while, and he didn't get why this was so difficult for me to understand.

Mike, making this passionate speech while some kid played an arcade game behind us, seemed angrier at me than he'd ever been. Enough time had passed since the beginning of our relationship that I was no longer limited to my instinctive reaction, which would have been to freeze any hint of emotion out of my face and look coldly at him without moving a muscle the whole time he was speaking and then, when he was finished, say, "Okay," and turn on my heel and leave, imagining a ~~meteor falling down from a clear sky to crush him~~ (no; not protracted enough) ~~violent explosion of something made of glass that sent tiny glass shards flying into every part of him, beginning with his eyes and making sure not to miss his genitalia~~ (no; even if he went blind the rest of him would heal eventually) creeping, leprous infection of a type contracted only by speaking sharply in movie theaters to people who didn't deserve it, an infection that both kept him in agonizing pain for years and deformed his countenance monstrously so that his outsides would reflect the rot that was in his soul, and he would be aware the entire time that this wouldn't be happening to him if he hadn't been so mean to me.

But, as I say, by this point my conflict-resolution skills had matured somewhat, so I was able to offer sincere apologies mixed with expressions of frustration at what I perceived as Mike's inflexibility and need to control things.

We made a sort of peace eventually and left the theater to go to the Barnes & Noble next door, where we browsed for an hour or so. I bought a couple books and a little box of four Godiva chocolates, which I started eating while we waited for the subway home. "Hey, can I have a bite?" asked Mike as he eyed the caramel-filled half piece of chocolate in my hand.

"No," I said.

"What?" he said, apparently taken aback. Then he decided I was kidding. "Funny. Give me a bite."

"No."

"Why not?" His eyes had narrowed.

"Are you serious? You just disemboweled me in public and you don't understand why I won't give you a bite of chocolate?"

"*Fine.*" He stalked a few yards over to lean against a pillar, and I stayed where I was, which meant that when the subway came we got into separate cars. I was fuming and I'm sure he was too. We walked home from our subway stop separately, which was the first time that had ever happened, and when we got home the first thing we did was have another, even bigger fight, this time about the kitchen.

Let us pause briefly while I explain the extent to which I am not a neat person.

It's not that I don't care. I really do like things beautiful and orderly and lined up and clean and sunshine and bluebirds and fabric softener, and I really wish I could keep them that way, but I can't.

The good news is that it's not my fault; I fell on my head as a baby.

"I told you to watch him!" my mother shrieked when she got back from lunch to see blood pouring out of my two-year-old scalp.

"I did!" said my father. "I did watch him! I watched him climb up on the sink, I watched him lose his balance, I watched him fall, I watched him hit his head. . . ."

For most of my life I thought that the one-inch-diameter bald spot on top of my head was my sole memento of the fall, but a few years ago, for reasons too tedious to go into here, I had a brain scan, and it turns out that *I'm brain damaged.* The part of my brain underneath the bald spot is sluggish, as is, to a lesser extent, the corresponding part on the other side. The first sluggish area, my doctor told me, is the section of the brain that processes visual information, which explains a great deal (why I had to stop playing video games in 1984 when they started coming out in 3D, because I found them overwhelming; why I hate art), and the second area is the section of the brain that governs organization, which also explains a great deal. So my tendency toward messiness isn't a fault; it's a disability—not only can't I organize things, I also can't see that I've neglected to organize them—for which I should receive special consideration and perhaps a parking space.

Mike, on the other hand, is a very organized person; he's also a very visual person, and decided to become a psychiatrist only after considering and rejecting the idea of becoming a painter. ("The ratio of success to starvation was way too low for me," he said.) So when I got home, having walked a block and a half behind him from the subway, it was only to be confronted with his fury in the kitchen. "You told me you were going to clean this up," he said hotly, indicating the counter, which had a great number of towering stacks of paper on it, along with several books and a half-empty tin of brownies. "You said that *two weeks ago*, and it's still a disaster. It's like you're not even aware that I exist. You know how anxious I get when things are messy, and all I can think is that you just don't fucking care."

"Oh, you mean like how I didn't care yesterday when you texted me that you were having a bad day at work and I went to get raspberries so I could make you peach Melba for dessert and I had to take the subway an hour each way to get them because you made us move into a ghetto in the middle of nowhere where they don't even sell raspberries? And like how I didn't care when I spent three hours writing those recommendations for your students on Thursday because you're just shy of dyslexic? You mean like *that* not caring?"

We went on like this for half an hour or so, and this time we didn't come to any sort of peace. Mike stormed upstairs and I decided that if he wanted a clean kitchen he was damn well going to get one. So I moved all the papers and books into my office, ate the remaining brownies, including the corners, which are Mike's favorites, and took everything else in the room, put it in garbage bags, and dragged it down to the basement. And by "everything" I mean *everything*. Not just the knife stand and the blender, so that the counter would be clear, but everything in the drawers and cabinets, too. Dishes, silverware, glasses. The ice cream maker. The colander. The Cuisinart. They all went into huge thirty-gallon trash bags. Pots, pans, pie dishes, cake tins, the citrus zester. And the pantry. Cereal, flour, honey, pasta, spices, extract of orange, baking powder, all of it. The delivery menus. The refrigerator magnets. I almost took the food in the fridge and freezer down but left it simply because sometimes when I can't sleep I eat instead and I didn't want to risk going down to the basement in the middle of the night and consuming a snack that had turned and getting salmonella.

And let me tell you, by the time I was done, that kitchen was fucking *clean*.

Altogether this took me an hour or two, at the end of which time, feeling very satisfied with myself, I went into my office, shut the door, and started making notes for a short story in which a cruel, sadistic psychiatrist is tortured and killed by the patients he has victimized.

It wasn't too long before I heard the sound of Mike coming down the stairs, followed by the sound of Mike going into the kitchen, followed by a short period of silence, followed by what might reasonably be termed the Door Slam Heard 'Round the World, followed by the sound of Mike storming back up the stairs. Then I went back to my notes for the story, realizing that I had neglected to include a scene in which the fiendish psychiatrist begs his victims to have mercy on him and they just laugh and laugh and bring out longer knives.

"I'm really sorry," I said in my voice mail message to Mike the next day.

"I was livid," he said in his answering voice mail message, "but to tell you the truth I was also kind of impressed. And I'm really sorry too."

Over the next few days I brought most of the kitchen stuff up from the basement and put it back. Some of it I left down there because we didn't really need it (I'm sure I had a very good reason for taking that handblown monstrosity of a candleholder off my friend Dave's hands when he was moving but I'll be damned if I can tell you what it was).

The problem was the lids for the pots and pans.

They were NOWHERE TO BE FOUND.

I swear to you, I scoured that basement for hours—days, months—looking for them, and they had vanished. Every once in a while during the next few years I looked for them again, but nothing doing. I'm not sure why it didn't occur to me to replace them; when I needed to cover a pot I just put a pan on top of it and vice versa, which was actually really inconvenient.

"Mike," asked Dr. Basescu, "do you understand what Joel is asking for when he says he wants you to be specific about how you'd like to be involved in planning the wedding?"

"But I *am* being specific," he answered. "I don't know how I can be *more* specific."

"All you'll say," I said, "is that you want me to take care of the details and check in with you about important things. But it's a mystery to me what you think is a detail and what you think is important, and you never tell me, and you get annoyed when I ask, so I've stopped asking, and I just have to guess, and I hate that."

"It should be obvious."

"Honey, when I say I've talked to Sugar Sweet Sunshine about getting cupcakes you get annoyed that I didn't ask you to taste them first, but then when I ask you to sit with me and make a list of who we want to invite you get annoyed and say we've already talked about it and I should just go ahead and invite them."

"That's because we *have* already talked about it, for *days*, and we made a list, which took us *hours*, and you *lost* it."

It was around this time that the couples therapist started asking me whether I understood what Mike was expressing.

I think that the historical event most damaging to the institution of marriage, far more than divorce or same-sexers getting married, may have been the birth of romance novelist Kathleen Thompson Norris in San Francisco on July 16, 1880. Upon her death in 1966, the *New York Times* described her as a militant feminist, but *Time* called her novels, which had sold over ten million copies, "relentlessly wholesome." In 1926, she published a book called *The Black Flemings*, about the tempestuous love between Gabrielle and David; on page 345 one reads the following words:

"'When I was away from him, I had time to think it out logically and dispassionately, and I knew he was—the one,' the girl resumed, 'and when I saw him—whenever we were together, although I couldn't think logically, or indeed think at all,' she said, laughing, and flushed, and meeting his eyes with a sort of defiant courage, 'I knew, from the way I felt, that there never could be, and never would be, any one else!'" (Page 345 of *The Black Flemings* also contains the line, "'But after I got home from Paris I saw him again,' the girl offered, lucidly." I feel that if somebody who writes like that can sell ten million books I am clearly going about this whole author thing in the wrong way.)

This is, in any case, the earliest instance I've been able to find of the use of the unmodified term "the one" as shorthand for something like "the person I'm meant to be with in a match made by destiny." The idea of love written in the stars has been around—well, really from the beginning, when God saw that Adam was lonely and knew just the companion to give him.

The One.

I love Mike, and I believe myself immeasurably lucky that he has allowed me (thus far, at least) to yoke my life to his. But every day I pass twenty men to whose lives I fantasize about yoking mine, and each one of them, in the moment I see him, is better than Mike; each of those twenty men, in the moment I see him, is The One, because Mike certainly isn't. He snores, he's rigid, he likes black-and-white movies. He's balding and he's a bad speller. He's full of energy during the day, only to come home from work listless and tired, whereas I'm listless and tired during the day, only to be full of energy in the evening, when all he wants to do is watch goddamn home and garden shows on HGTV. He nags me to eat vegetables. He makes me come along with him on trips to Home Depot. In the drugstore he stands paralyzed for minutes at a time, two minutes, five minutes, unable to decide whether to buy the Dove soap for $1.29 or the less appealing Ivory Spring soap for $1.19. He rises early on the weekend and gets grumpy when I want him to spend time lazing in bed with me. If we're having a conversation walking down the street he is constantly distracted by architecture.

None of the possible Ones upon whom my glance falls on any given day has any of these faults. The brunet standing in the 2 train reading *Go Ask Alice* has the same circadian rhythms as I do and would rush to any movie about a) sorcerers and/or dragons, b) aliens who try to destroy the earth, c) a college student whose roommate begins exhibiting strange behavior the day after fooling around with a Ouija board, and/or d) a guy who gets kidnapped by a top-secret counterintelligence agency and transformed into a powerful force for destruction but escapes to become a sword-wielding angel of vengeance and woe betide them who first disturbed his peaceful, ordinary life. The blond sitting across from me on the 5 train (I transferred at Franklin Avenue) playing a game on his iPad won't sulk when I tell him I'm not interested in puttering around in the garden with him and doesn't see the need to pressure decent, self-respecting people to eat broccoli. The stocky man in a shirt and tie walking three strides ahead of me down 14th Street toward Trader Joe's doesn't even *subscribe* to

HGTV, much less spend all his time watching it, he prefers going to the hardware store alone, and he can choose a soap without even stopping the cart.

Then of course there's my Facebook friend Eric, who spells well, who isn't losing his hair, and whose engorged penis, I can see from the picture he emailed me the day we were sending flirty messages back and forth, is not only larger than Mike's and larger than mine but larger than Mike's and mine put together and in fact larger than any engorged penis it has ever been my privilege to behold. And Matt, whose blog's air of weary, threadbare irony is far more eloquent than anything Mike could write and who proved, when I met him in London, to be gorgeous, and if only I'd known that he and his partner weren't monogamous I could have had one last glorious affair before starting to date Mike, and somehow Matt and I would both have realized that we were meant to be together and he would have dumped his partner and I would have moved to London or he would have moved here and my life would be perfect, and then of course that blond guy in Italy who caught my eye in the town square and beckoned me over but when I got to his table and his friend looked up at me expectantly I couldn't come up with anything to say so I pretended I'd thought he was somebody else and went and sat in a corner of the cafe hoping against hope that he'd pass by on his way out but he didn't and I lost my one chance at true happiness.

(And don't forget Cole, beautiful, perfect Cole, my new husband, but we've already discussed him.)

Every one of these men would be a better husband than Mike; each would support me in ways that Mike could never even understand, would satisfy needs Mike isn't even aware I have.

There are just two problems with this.

The first problem is that these men don't exist.

The second problem is that, even if they did, they would be terribly, terribly wrong for me.

Take the brunet reading *Go Ask Alice*. I've already revealed that we share biorhythms and a taste in movies. Let's be generous and say he prefers to be alone when gardening or going to the hardware store, takes a dim view of vegetables, has never watched HGTV, can make hygiene-product decisions faster than Mitt Romney changes political positions, spells well, and has a cock that would give Catherine the Great pause.

The thing is, you can't play connect the dots with only eleven data points. Or, rather, you can, but your chances of getting the right image are pretty slim. Take these dots, for example:

I can look at them and see this:

And I can fantasize and dream about it and know with absolute certainty that I've found the apple of my dreams, when in fact the dots actually connect to form this:

You take my point: All I actually know about the brunet is that he's handsome and has attractively ironic taste in literature. The rest of it I'm making up out of whole cloth—an unfortunate example of something that psychologists, if I understand correctly, call the halo effect, whereby humans assume, because we've evolved to draw broad inferences from whatever data we're presented with, that attractive people are also smart, kind, fun, interesting, and good in bed. I want an apple, so when I see the dots Mr. *Go Ask Alice* presents, it's easy for me to connect them to make an apple, when in fact I have no idea whether he's an apple or a bottle of poison. Or, for that matter, a choo-choo train, a Finno-Ugric linguist, despair, the Principality of Andorra, Yggdrasil (the World Tree of Norse myth), Fyodor Dostoevsky, a bacon double cheeseburger, the molecular structure of hydrochloric acid, or dirt. In fact the chances that he's an apple are so low as to be, for all practical intents and purposes, zero.

Or are they?

If there are seven billion people on earth, roughly half of whom are men, roughly 65 percent of whom are between the ages of fifteen and sixty-four (I am neither a pedophile nor a grandpa chaser, but those are the ages that bound the most appropriate category in the *CIA World Factbook*), roughly 5 percent of whom, according to the Williams Institute on Sexual Orientation Law, might identify as gay—the old one-in-ten statistic, it turns out, was a little optimistic—then the chances that my soul mate is the brunet (who proves upon further examination to have a cute scar above his eyebrow; is he Harry Potter?) are something like 1 in 111,743,043.

Not lottery-ticket-purchasing odds.

But I doubt that even dropping the arch act and admitting that people who say "The One" don't really mean "the one person on earth who is my soul mate" but "a person who's perfect for me" or "a person who satisfies all my needs" or "a person who meets every requirement on my checklist" makes the odds a whole lot better. Because it's really difficult for me to imagine that such a person can exist. I've dated guys who seemed to be The One whom I later had to dump because they turned out to be racists, or bad spellers, or bottoms like me ("What are you going to do," my friend Stephen asked, "get together and bump pussies?"), or Republicans, or one or several of any number of other undesirable attributes that put them out of the running. Of course after dumping them I added their missing qualities to my list, but somehow the men I went out with seemed never to run out of new ways to disappoint me.

It's entirely possible that I'm wrong and that the stocky man in a shirt and tie walking three strides ahead of me down 14th Street toward Trader Joe's would in fact have been the perfect man as I see him. I'm at something of a loss here, because when I talked about this in my last book I think I got it exactly right, and I don't want to gild the lily, but at the same time it's relevant to the discussion, so the best I can do is quote myself, *à la* Jonah Lehrer, and say that, if I had gone up to him and tapped him on the shoulder and managed to charm him with my self-conscious flirting, Mr. Stocky might well have turned out to be "gorgeous, hysterically funny, a towering genius, a master of sparkling repartee, fabulously wealthy, blond, multilingual (my dream was that he would speak eight languages but I [would be] willing to settle for five, as long as he could punctuate correctly in all of them), and possessed of beautifully shaped teeth. I wouldn't even have to trick him into thinking that I was just as perfect as he was, because simply being with him would wipe out my faults as utterly as if they were the city of Carthage or Jennifer Grey's old nose."

But statistically, it seems much more likely that he would have turned out to be a racist Republican bottom who couldn't spell.

"I'm willing to wait until I meet a man who's exactly right," said a friend of mine when we were talking about this a few years ago.

"That's fine," I said, "but I think you're going to die alone."

I don't know. There's no way for me to find out whether I'm right or not (not that I usually let that get in my way). So I could be spending this entire book justifying having made the wrong choice. I could be spending my entire *life*, for that matter, justifying having made the wrong choice. But I have to imagine that, once Cinderella and the Prince had been together for five or six years, he got pretty sick of her snoring, and she had come to hate the way he talked incessantly about the flora and fauna of whatever enchanted forest they were passing through, and every once in a while she burped or he farted, and they continually disappointed each other and neither one of them was ever truly everything that the other wanted.

And I guess the reason I believe this is that, when I think about The One and when I run down my checklist, sometimes making adjustments to it (no, I've actually realized that the requirement that he cry at the same time as me at the movies is *more* important than the requirement that he share my fantasy that one day they're able to reconstruct the ancient Library of Alexandria and all its manuscripts), I feel like what I'm developing a picture of is not the perfect spouse but the perfect self, somebody who has all of my virtues and none of my flaws. Yesterday I tried to put on a pair of shorts I bought two years ago and I couldn't fit into them, but if my husband, Mr. The One, has a perfect body, then who'll notice? I end up in situations every day in which I have no idea what to do or say and end up stammering out something completely in-appropriate that does nothing but embarrass me hideously, but if my husband is actually foreign royalty and has been trained to know what to do or say no matter what the circumstances, then I won't have to face my own insufficiency. I only pretend to have read most of what I say I've read, but if I'm married to a man who's read it all then it won't matter, because I can just ask him and he'll tell me and the end result will be the same.

And I'm not a psychologist, but I can't believe such a relation-ship would be healthy. Because if what you're looking for isn't a partner but a completion, well, you're destined to fail, because nobody gets to be complete. Sorry. Game over. All your base are belong to us. I may see the world through thorn-colored glasses, but, in a society that allows Michael Brown, former head of the Federal Emergency Management Agency, whose flagitious response after Hurricane Katrina to a desperate plea for food, water, and medical services for the 30,000 people in the Louisiana Superdome was an email that read, "Thanks for the update. Anything specific I need to do or tweak?," to make six figures a year as a speaker about disaster preparedness, an equation that aims for wholeness requires a more complicated calculus than Disney can design.

But if Mr. The One is not the spouse we all ought to have, then who is?

"I just feel so much *pressure* from you all the time," said Mike, as Dr. Basescu looked compassionately on. "It's like, we talk about maybe doing something, and then you're in my face saying, 'Let's do it NOW NOW NOW NOW NOW.' With everything, not just the wedding planning. But the wedding planning is a good example. Like the ketubah. You're so *insistent* about it, I wish you'd just leave me alone."

"The reason I feel like I have to be in your face saying NOW is that otherwise you'll never make a decision. We say, we need to get a ketubah, and then I keep asking about it, and you say, oh, let's figure it out later, and then when I ask about it later you say, oh, let's figure it out later, and then it's too late. So if we want a ketubah I feel like I *have* to keep annoying you about it or we'll end up without one."

"It sounds to me," said Dr. Basescu, "as if one of the issues you guys are facing is that you have different starting speeds. Joel, you go from zero to sixty in one second, and Mike, you take a while to get there. So when Joel tries to make you as a couple go faster, you feel like he's dragging you more quickly than you feel comfortable with, and Joel, when Mike tries to make you as a couple go slower, you feel like he's putting the brakes on and keeping you from going anywhere."

"Wow," I said. "That's incredibly insightful."

"Yeah," said Mike, "it helps a lot to see it that way." He turned to me, his face filled with relief. "So you just have to slow down and our wedding will be fine!"

"Um, no, you have to speed up and our wedding will be fine. So what are we doing about a ketubah NOW NOW NOW NOW NOW?"

"Can you guys understand how it might be difficult to hear what you're asking each other?"

This is what I learned in couples therapy: marriage is hard work.

You paid somebody $125 a week to tell you that?, I can hear you thinking. *Why not just stop by the self-help section of the nearest bookstore, close your eyes and spin around, and buy whatever collection of pabulum you end up pointing at?*

I understand. I've been hearing that marriage is hard work since before I imagined that marriage was a possibility for me. I get it. Marriage is hard work.

But the people who say this are leaving out the most important part; they're lying by omission. The idea that marriage is hard work never bothered me in the slightest, because I work hard. I work really hard. Really, *really* hard. I wrote and cut more songs from my last musical than actually ended up in the musical. I edit drafts of my writing as if they were crystal meth. Back when I was blogging regularly I could easily spend three hours on a two-paragraph post.

No, the part that people leave out is that marriage is hard work of a kind that makes you incredibly uncomfortable to do.

Marriage is hard work like understanding that, when you ask your husband on Saturday afternoon whether he wants to go to the theater with your friends on Thursday and he tells you he'll think about it, and then he never says anything about it, and then when you ask him again on Tuesday morning he says can we talk about it tonight, and by the time you actually pin him down your friends have already bought their tickets and you have to spend Thursday night in front of the television watching season two of *Dollhouse* on Netflix, it's not because he doesn't want to go but can't bring himself to say no, it's not because he doesn't like your friends, it's not because he wants to make your life miserable though somehow he's succeeding, it's because having to make decisions overwhelms him and you need to find a different way to ask him.

Hard work like realizing that it's not enough to go on the neighborhood tour with him; you have to take an actual interest in the fact that the house at 127 was designed by the same architect as the house at 142 but ten years later and look how he evolved, even though you don't care and can't tell the difference, or he'll feel like he's doing it alone. And faking it doesn't work.

Hard work like watching his goddamn home and garden shows with him.

And, conversely, marriage is also hard work like remembering, as you walk down the street, even though really all you can think about is which politicians you'd kill first if you got turned into a werewolf and could do so with impunity, or how the hell Julianna Margulies is going to get out of the imbroglio she's gotten herself into on *The Good Wife*, that you promised a couple days ago you'd get your husband a new pair of nail clippers because he got upset when you used his, and keeping an eye out for a Duane Reade because, even though the pair he has is working just fine, and given the parts of him that have been in the parts of you the idea of not wanting to share nail clippers is ridiculous, and there's no reason at all this can't wait until you remember it later, if you come home without the damn nail clippers he's going to feel like he doesn't matter to you.

Hard work like spending all day in your house without talking to a single person but having made excellent progress on a piece you're working on and then realizing, when he comes home from a terrible day at work, that there's only a certain amount of emotional energy he has left and it's not enough for this, and stifling your excitement to tell him all about it.

Like saying to him after dinner that you'll be upstairs in five minutes and then catching sight of an *amazing* piece online about Johannes Kepler, father of optometry and author of the laws of planetary motion, and still making it upstairs within fifteen minutes instead of an hour, even though it means leaving unfinished the account of how Kepler was actually a *sociopath* who *murdered* his mentor, Tycho Brahe, and even though the piece about Kepler's sociopathy opens up previously unimaginable vistas of thought and creation and hilarity, while going upstairs just means you have yet another conversation with your husband about what to do with the dogs when you leave for vacation.

And that's the thing. I can bake pie upon pie upon pie for my husband, and I can write letter of recommendation after letter of recommendation for his students, and I can search for hours on end for the perfect dinnerware to replace the dinnerware I brought into the marriage, which he hates, because, despite the fact that those things all take hard work of one kind or another, I enjoy doing that work.

When I'm trying to make lists of lycanthropic assassination targets or figure out how Julianna Margulies is going to rescue herself on *The Good Wife*, keeping an eye out for a Duane Reade only gets in my way.

So I guess that's what the "marriage is hard work" people are leaving out: marriage isn't just hard work. Marriage is hard work that *gets in your way*.

No wonder 50 percent of married people have affairs.

There are a lot of different positions gay couples can take on monogamy: We're monogamous. We can sleep with other people but only if we tell each other about it. We can sleep with other people but only if we *don't* tell each other about it. We can sleep with other people but only if we take pictures. We can sleep with other people when we're not in the same city. We can sleep with other people but not in our home. We can sleep with other people but only when we do it together. We can sleep with other people as long as we avoid certain sexual activities. We can sleep with other people but nobody more than once. We can sleep with other people but only infrequently. We can sleep with other people with no restrictions. (Of course there's also the fact that either member of a couple can choose to abide or not to abide by the terms agreed upon.)

So monogamy is a really tricky thing to talk about, at least among gay men. Or, rather, it's not so tricky to talk about among gay men, but it's tricky to talk about among gay men if straight people are listening, because the cultural standards are simply different—our inability to marry each other has to play into this—and there simply isn't as strong a belief, as there seems to be in straight society, that monogamy is the only way to get a relationship right. I think much of this has to do with the fact that gay male couples are made up of two men, each of whom understands that it's a struggle for the other to get anything done in life at all given the strength of his desire to bed every halfway attractive man who walks by. In straight couples, it's a struggle for the man to get anything done in life given the strength of his desire to bed every halfway attractive woman who walks by, but his partner has little personal insight into this feeling, and whether she understands or not he usually doesn't think she does, so things get complicated.

Of course, it's much simpler in the rest of the animal kingdom. It turns out that even the much-vaunted monogamy of the prairie vole is a myth, at least in the way monogamy advocates talk about it. The only examples of absolute sexual monogamy I could find in the animal kingdom were a) the urban coyote and b) several species in which, after they mate, the female kills the male. Monogamy is unnatural and probably stupid.

Nevertheless, Mike and I have decided to be monogamous, and since the day I made a commitment to him I haven't slept with anybody else. For all I know he may have turned his office at the hospital's department of psychiatry into a lurid cavern of venial delights, but given his schedule I suspect it's unlikely. I think we talked for like a minute and a half once, early in our relationship, about the idea of having threesomes as a couple, but even then our hearts weren't really in it.

For me it was easy to choose monogamy, for a very simple reason: I'm way too insecure for anything else. If Mike and I decided that playing around was okay, I would spend every single moment I wasn't with him obsessing over who he might be with, into what orifices he might be inserting what turgid body parts, and in what ways he might prefer which partner(s) to me. I would become so shrill a harpy that Petruchio, come to wive it wealthily in Padua, would take one look at me and go home. "So, honey," I would say very casually when Mike came through the door at 6:17, "I see that it took you twelve minutes longer than usual to get home from the hospital. Is there anything you want to tell me?" And when he said no I would say, "*Really?* Are you *absolutely certain?* Because I called you and got your voice mail and it's difficult for me to believe that . . ." and so on and so on through hissed accusations all the way to shouting and ostentatious silences and we would break up before the week was out.

I suppose the other alternative would be for me to sleep around without Mike's permission and not tell him, but that, too, would render me practically nonfunctional, because doing something I'm not supposed to do and then trying to keep it a secret sends me into a dazed state that would give Oliver Sacks enough material for a new book. My entire life begins to revolve around my transgression and my world becomes narrower and narrower and narrower until finally the secret becomes the only thing that exists, preventing me ultimately from even chewing food.

So what's left is monogamy, no matter how stupid and unnatural it is.

As the years have passed, however, I find that I have another reason not to sleep with anybody else.

We in twenty-first-century America have burdened marriage with much more weight than it has ever had to bear.

Until a couple centuries ago, marriage as we know it tended to be a business arrangement. In the upper classes, wives were for bearing children and cementing political alliances; for love, a man had a mistress, or several. (Women took lovers too, of course, but these arrangements were less sanctioned by society, given that, by creating uncertainty in questions of paternity, they threatened the passing of property from a father to his son.) In the lower classes, men and women were essentially corporate partners, because to plow the field, milk the cow, feed the children, *and* mend the clothing was simply beyond the ability of one person. One presumes that the lower classes had extramarital flings as well, but since they rarely featured in broadsheets we have much less information about them. The point is: for most of our history, monogamy has been an incidental part of marriage at best.

I suspect that it was in 1848 that this began to change in America, with the passage in New York State of the Married Women's Property Act, which decreed that women who came into marriage with property could keep it instead of automatically giving up ownership to their husbands. This meant that, if a man married a rich woman, he could no longer take his right to do what he liked with her property for granted, and married women gained a degree of power thitherto, I believe, unknown to them. (When I asked Stephanie Coontz, author of *Marriage, a History*, she wasn't so specific as to name a particular date or law, but she said I had the right idea; she added that the change in attitude toward monogamy continued in the twentieth century with the wider availability of divorce and contraception, aided by the increasing importance of what she called "the love match.") Society had never stopped turning a blind eye to men who had extra-marital sex and frowning on women who did the same, it's true, but with the Married Women's Property Act women were finally in a position to do something about the double standard. Either they should be allowed to have affairs too, or their husbands should be forbidden to do so. Since the first option required abandoning the basic principles of inheritance—if your wife could sleep with other people then how did you know you were leaving your property to your own son and not somebody else's?—men had to get a lot more discreet about their mistresses if they ever wanted access to their wives' money again.

As a result, the only person left to love with the approval of society was your spouse.

And nobody noticed it, but since then marriage has had to carry the double load of work and love. And that's some heavy cargo.

Because really the old arrangement made a lot of sense, at least for those who profited by it. Gay men have just been more honest about it; my understanding is that roughly a third of gay male couples are monogamous, a third claim to be monogamous but one partner or the other cheats (or both), and a third are either explicitly non-monogamous or what author and sex columnist Dan Savage brilliantly calls *monogamish*. (Of course there are non-monogamous straight and lesbian couples too, but either there are fewer of them or they're more discreet.)

I have no stake in other people's decisions about monogamy. Secretly I feel smug and superior to men in non-monogamous couples but even I know there's no justification for this feeling; I just seize every opportunity I can to feel smug and superior. I suppose I take a dim view of cheating, but really what business is it of mine what anybody else tells or doesn't tell his husband?

I've realized, though, that, for me at any rate, there's a very good argument in favor of monogamy, which is: I want to guarantee my emotional intimacy with Mike. And if he's my sole sexual outlet—if monogamy has cut off any other options—then I'll have to maintain emotional intimacy in order to satisfy the fundamental human need for sex. If he does something obnoxious and plants thereby a tiny seed of resentment in me that grows slowly into something hale and poisonously healthy, then if I can have sex with other people I'm just going to continue resenting him and go off and have sex with whoever until that resentment becomes a mighty, poisonous oak that I'll never be able to chop down, and I'll just keep having sex with other people and that tree will always be there and I'll never feel close to him again. (I'm working here on the assumption that it's not possible to sustain willingly a long-term sexual relationship with somebody toward whom your strongest feeling is resentment.)

Obviously it's possible to bridge distance and uproot resentment in the absence of monogamy. But I'm so frightened of conflict that I can easily see doing nothing about the situation and growing old in a loveless, lonely marriage and being miserable until I die.

So if that's the alternative, then eliminating all options except the one that forces me to maintain an emotional closeness with Mike seems the obvious choice.

Not that that makes it easy. And of course, I don't know whether monogamy is the chicken or the egg in this situation. Those fantasies I begin to spin when I see a potential The One aren't just emotional, and sometimes when one of The Ones notices me shifting to cover the physical component of my fantasies he smiles at me in such a way as to make it clear that I needn't do so on his account, and very occasionally he even suggests that we do something about it. (I don't mean to suggest that men throw themselves at me wherever I go, which is certainly not the case, but I *do* live in New York City, after all.) After Mike's father died and he and I were growing more and more distant because of that whore the television, my Facebook chats with my friend Eric (he of the giant penis), who is gorgeous and smart and sweet and who has made no secret of his desire to sleep with me, got longer and longer, and when I had to take a trip to the city where he lives I couldn't keep myself from asking him whether he had an extra bed. Luckily he said he'd be out of town while I was there; I'm fairly sure I wouldn't have ended up sleeping with him, especially because we have conflicting preferences in a certain question of practice, but I was also fairly sure I wouldn't break my left hand when I tried to do a flip back when I was on the gay cheerleading squad in my twenties, and look how that turned out.

Ultimately, though, I can't help noticing that the level of my temptation to take advantage of any given opportunity to be monogamish instead of monogamous usually correlates very directly with how close I'm feeling to Mike at the time. And I guess what keeps me on course is the understanding that the part of me that feels empty is not the part giving in to temptation would fill.

The day finally came in couples therapy when we reached the central issue in our relationship, or at least what I saw at the time as the central issue. (I still believe what I said before, that many of my fights with Mike could be avoided by his not being an asshole, but I think that's actually a side effect.)

"You're so goddamn self-sufficient," I said to Mike. And I realized that was it. "You won't let me in. And if you don't leave any room for me to support you emotionally, then eventually I stop trying."

"*What?*" he said. "I *have* to be emotionally self-sufficient, because if I don't support myself completely, *you* certainly aren't around to do it. You're too busy worrying about your damn ketubah."

"I suspect," said Dr. Basescu, "that we're looking at a vicious circle."

And I think this is the one problem that, according to Mike's friend Tony, our relationship has; everything else boils down in the end to this. Mike will have a particularly busy two weeks at work and I'll feel shut out, so I'll stop paying attention to him. Then he'll feel ignored, so he'll become seemingly self-sufficient, meeting all his own needs. This self-sufficiency makes me feel further shut out in turn, which makes me stop paying attention to him, which makes him feel further ignored, which makes . . .

This is, Dr. Basescu helped us realize, what was going on after Mike's father died. If I could have supported him, he could have let me in. If he could have let me in, I could have supported him. But we couldn't.

Since discovering the issue we've gotten a little better at noticing when this happens and pointing it out to each other so we can step back from it and let it go its merry way, but when we're in the middle of the fray, we can be rendered even today so incapable of real communication that we might as well be living in the Pliocene Epoch, before human beings developed language. Here are some examples.

What I say: "Honey, come in here and hang out on the couch with me."

What I'm thinking: "What if he says no? That would mean I've chosen to spend my life with somebody who doesn't even want to spend time with me, and whereas before I was alone with the potential to meet a life partner, now I *have* a life partner and I'm *still* alone."

What he hears: "I *demand* that you abandon whatever you're doing, come here *this instant*, and hang out on the couch with me."

What I say: "What's on your mind?"

What I'm thinking: "He's quieter than usual. Is he mad at me about something? What is he mad at me for? If I can figure it out then I can apologize before he tells me and then I'll get credit for knowing what it was *and* apologizing before he even says anything."

What he hears: "I don't care that you're worried about your mother; I'm more important."

What I say: "What are you ordering [from the menu]?"

What I'm thinking: "Is he going to get a margarita or not? Alcohol makes him fall asleep the instant he gets in bed, so if he gets a margarita then I know we're not having sex tonight and we haven't had sex in like forever so if he gets a margarita then obviously it's because he's not attracted to me anymore."

What he hears: "Will you hurry up and make a fucking *decision* already?"

"Oh, are you looking at pictures of your new husband Cole again?" asked Mike as he passed by a few minutes ago.

"No," I said. "Cole is a hateful, hateful blackguard and he and I are no longer married."

"Why?"

"It was my fault. I saw him in another reading and left yet another Facebook post on his wall about how great his performance was."

"Well, that was desperate."

"Yeah, which I realized about one second after I clicked send. And then I proved myself to be even *more* desperate by messaging him when I saw him online and was like, hey, you were great the other day, and he was like, I did see your wall post, and I was like, something stupid, and he was like, something forbearing, and I was like, something even stupider, and he was like, isn't the weather great, and I knew what we'd had was gone forever."

"You want me to rough him up?"

"No, that's okay. I'm married to Nick now."

"Let me see." He moved to look over my shoulder. "You and your bland blonds."

"You're just jealous."

"No, 'cause you don't really love him."

"I do, too!" I said. "As a matter of fact, he's on his way over right now."

"Okay," said Mike. "So we shouldn't waste the time we've got left."

"It should take him about an hour," I said.

"Oh, but my new husband Jonathan will be here before then."

"Well, we've had a nice run, haven't we?"

"Nothing to be ashamed of."

"Wanna go see *The Avengers*?"

"Sure. Let me get my keys."

"But what will happen when Nick and Jonathan get here and we're gone?"

"They'll find something to do."

8

Taking Care
of Last-Minute Details

Saturday, September 11

One month from today, I am getting married to my boyfriend of seven years. I suspect I would feel much more nervous than I do if it weren't for the fact that all my energy is taken up by the HGTV Urban Oasis Giveaway, which is in the grand scheme of things at least as important to me as my wedding, if not more.

Because I hate living in Brooklyn. Our house is in an area populated largely by people from the Caribbean, the downside of which is that the restaurants tend to serve a lot of goat, when what I want instead is a really first-rate Taco Bell. While the crack dealers on our right have come to love me—they call me Jimmy, after Clark Kent's sidekick Jimmy Olsen, and I am supremely confident that if anybody tried to mess with me I could go to the crack dealers and ask them to intervene on my behalf and somebody would end up looking down the wrong end of a sawed-off shotgun—and the retired schoolteacher on our left has calmed down quite a bit, I would feel the same way if I lived in a posh neighborhood like Park Slope or Brooklyn Heights, because I believe, with the utmost provinciality, that Manhattan is the center of the world, which means I'm living in a suburb of the center of the world, and why would anybody do that?

(If anything, the fact that my neighborhood is a ghetto makes it better than Park Slope or Brooklyn Heights, simply because it's more interesting. Though the gunfire we used to hear once a week has slowed down, thanks to gentrification, to once every few months, and though I will never forgive Mike for not calling me at once so I could join him when on his way to the grocery store he walked by the body of the guy who had been stabbed to death, telling people where I live still produces a dismayed response often enough for me to enjoy doing so. Nonetheless, since the police crackdown that led the Crips to abandon our corner store as a hangout and move to a different corner more than two blocks away from the Bloods hangout, things haven't been the same.)

All the hours I have put in watching Mike's goddamn home and garden television shows with him, however, have now presented me with an alternative. HGTV is giving away an apartment in downtown Manhattan, designed and furnished by none other than Mr. Vern Yip himself, the only halfway decent designer from *Trading Spaces* and now one of the judges on *Design Star*. The apartment, which is in the Residences at the W Hotel on Washington Street, has an area of 800-some-odd square feet and an astonishing view of the Statue of Liberty.

You're allowed to enter the giveaway once a day online, at hgtv.com. I read the small print, however, and it turns out that the once-a-day rule applies only to online entries and that, if you enter by mail, sending an index card with your name, address, birthday, phone number, and social security number handwritten on it in a hand-addressed, hand-stamped envelope to the HGTV post office box in Tennessee, you're allowed to enter as many times as you like.

So yesterday I went out and bought five thousand index cards and five thousand envelopes, which means that by the time I leave for my honeymoon—four days before the HGTV Urban Oasis Giveaway deadline—I'm going to know my mailing address very, very well.

HGTV Urban Oasis Giveaway cards left to fill out: 5,000.
HGTV Urban Oasis Giveaway envelopes left to address: 5,000.

Sunday, September 12

In order to start hand-writing entries for the HGTV Urban Oasis Giveaway I first need to finish hand-writing the wedding invitations and then mail them. They're a formality, as we already know who's coming and who isn't, but if I didn't send them I would feel incorrect.

The pleasure of your company is requested
at the marriage of
Joel Legare Derfner
to
Michael David Combs
on Sunday, the tenth of October, nine o'clock in the morning
at the Brooklyn Botanic Garden.

I hope I'll be able to find a Julius and Ethel Rosenberg stamp or a J. Robert Oppenheimer stamp or something like that but I worry that my tendency toward sentiment will lead me to choose the LOVE stamp.

HGTV Urban Oasis Giveaway cards left to fill out: 5,000.

HGTV Urban Oasis Giveaway envelopes left to address: 5,000.

Monday, September 13

"There were no Julius and Ethel Rosenberg stamps or J. Robert Oppenheimer stamps at the post office," I said to Mike.

"I'm sorry, honey," he said. "But I think the LOVE stamp will be sweet."

"No, I stayed strong. No LOVE stamp. Doris Miller. See?" I showed him the stamps I had bought.

"Who's that?"

"He joined the Navy but because he was black he had to be a cook or something. Then he grabbed a gun at Pearl Harbor and ended up shooting down like six Japanese planes and being awarded the Navy's version of the Purple Heart."

"Oh, that's nice. You couldn't manage McCarthyism or the atom bomb, but at least you got racism."

HGTV Urban Oasis Giveaway cards left to fill out: 4,923.

HGTV Urban Oasis Giveaway envelopes left to address: 4,923.

Tuesday, September 14

Rabbi Rachel has emailed us a Wikileaks' scandal worth of documents about wedding decisions we have to make, which we are taking one item at a time, starting with the list she's given us of things people say instead of "Behold, you are consecrated to me with this ring according to the law of Moses and Israel."

I will espouse (betroth) thee unto me forever. I will espouse (betroth) thee unto me in righteousness, and in lovingkindness and in compassion. And I shall betroth thee unto me in faithfulness.

Unacceptable. First of all, why do "forever" and "in faithfulness" get their own sentence, but "righteousness," "lovingkindness," and "compassion" all have to share one little espouse (betroth)? Also, the second sentence needs a serial comma.

By this ring you are consecrated to me as my husband.

That's just taking out "by the law of Moses and Israel" but pretending you didn't.

Fair is the white star of twilight, and the sky clearer at the day's end; but you are fairer, and you are dearer, you, my heart's friend.

Even Mike thinks this one is gross.

Many waters cannot quench love; neither can the floods drown it.

We're not getting married in scuba gear. More important, though, is the fact that love is about the relationship between two people, whereas marriage is about the relationship between them and society. Using "many waters cannot quench love" feels, oddly, too personal for a wedding ceremony. My love for Mike and his for me is nobody else's business, not even our wedding guests'.

I hope Rachel has a backup list.

Mike has rejected every single ketubah I've shown him.

HGTV Urban Oasis Giveaway cards left to fill out: 4,864.

HGTV Urban Oasis Giveaway envelopes left to address: 4,864.

Wednesday, September 15

I've told Mike that, since he's paying for the caterer, the cake, the Brooklyn Botanic Garden, and the rental of the morning clothes, I'll pay for the honeymoon.

The problem is that the travel agent I gave the deposit to said that the rest of the fee needs to be paid by a week from today, and right now, having paid the deposit and bought the HGTV Urban Oasis Giveaway cards and envelopes, I don't have the money to buy a pack of gum, much less a trip to the Caribbean.

Whatever. I'm sure some publisher will call me at the last minute to offer me a huge advance for my next book. Or maybe some producer will call me at the last minute to offer me a huge advance for my next show.

I would ask 28 for help, except I'm sure all he would say is that the money will appear when I'm ready for it.

HGTV Urban Oasis Giveaway cards left to fill out: 4,800.

HGTV Urban Oasis Giveaway envelopes left to address: 4,800.

Thursday, September 16

Why am I thinking of myself as the wife? There's no doubt that I am. When Rachel was telling us about the customs of a Jewish wedding, *I* was the one who didn't want to wear the veil—the idea that Mike could accept or reject a veil never occurred to me. And no way was I ever going to propose to Mike; I told him he had to propose to me. I'm the bride here. I don't know how to say this without opening up a huge can of worms, so I guess I should steel myself for a session of annelidology: I want to be the girl.

Of course I don't mean this in a literal sense. Homosexuality isn't, as a rule, about somebody being the boy and somebody being the girl. I'm a boy, Mike is a boy, we're both boys, and that's what allows us to be attracted to each other. We both identify as men. I still remember vividly the shudder of revulsion I felt when my now ex-boyfriend put on a dress and did a striptease—revulsion so strong it had to come from more than just the fact that I'm not attracted to women.

I am also aware of how easy it is for me as a man to talk about wanting to be "the girl" in a society that discriminates against women in employment, health care, and innumerable other facets of daily life. ("Take the pay cut to the seventy-seven cents a woman makes per dollar a man makes," said a friend of mine when I brought the idea up with her, "and then we'll talk.")

So what do I mean when I say I want to be the girl?

Unfortunately, I'm not exactly sure.

Am I talking about getting to be taken care of? About being put on a pedestal, about being cherished? About getting to be the special one?

And why are the things that occur to me entirely about benefits and not at all about responsibilities?

Perhaps there's something about being permitted to express your emotions?

In my last relationship, I suppose I was the boy and I thought of Tom as the girl. I was going to propose to him. Our relationship dynamic allowed him to be more emotionally expressive than I was. Maybe that was why we were so miserable. Maybe he really longed to be the boy. More likely we both longed to be the girl.

My therapist thinks it has to do with wanting to be wanted. My parents were more interested in saving the world than in paying attention to me, so now I'm trying to make up for it by being the one to whom attention ought to be paid.

Actually, that would explain my towering narcissism, too.

But seriously? I need what I need in my relationship with my fiancé because of what happened when I was eight?

Suspecting that the same sort of dynamic might operate in the relationships of other same-sexers, I posted a Facebook status update requesting my friends' thoughts on the issue. I got a number of "That's dumb, if somebody needs there to be a boy and a girl he should marry a girl"s and an even greater number of "blah blah blah offensive, patriarchal construct blah blah blah"s. Of course gender roles *are* an offensive, patriarchal construct, but I was after descriptions of an inner, emotional perspective.

Of those whose responses dealt with what I was investigating, a few people said it wasn't part of their experience at all. But they were a minority. Here are some of the replies I got from others.

"I view us both as two men with a broad array of emotions and tendencies. We equally share responsibility for the household finances, upkeep, etc. . . . We're both excellent cooks so we alternate chef duties. He's definitely a better housekeeper so he tends to do more of that just so that he won't have to live in my disarray. It may tip one way or the other at times with someone taking on more responsibility than is fair, but in the end, the other knows that he 'owes' the relationship some payback and it will be his time to take on some of the finances for both, yadda, yadda, yadda."

"In my relationship we're relatively balanced but I carry a bit more of the male energy. My past relationships have failed because I either carried too much of it or not enough of it in relation to my partner. I'm blessed to have found my perfect match!"

"While I don't want to be 'the girl,' I do like to think of my partner as 'the man.' Ours aren't traditional roles, but I'll happily cook for and feed my man, so long as he likes to do the directions and driving. (And it's always a little mixy because I'm so handy and will build all the Ikea, dig and plant a flower garden, and lay/grout a new tile or marble floor. . . .)"

"I actually often think about this, and more often than not it fills me with anxiety for some reason. I've been in long relationships with women in the past, have not been so lucky with men. There is a definite 'role' one plays when in a relationship and it kind of helps keep things on track and running smoothly. Once roles are switched up, it can lead to confusion and sometimes insecurity in my opinion. But labels only limit us, and allow others to feel comfort in thinking that everything has its place. The un-known, uncategorized, and unfamiliar will always be frightening. While labeling is limiting, I find freedom in playing any role that I feel like in that moment. Today, I feel like a garden gnome."

"I tend to see myself as the boy, because I like to be everything that is brought to mind when a man is in an opposite-sex relation-ship. I tend to be a protector, pay for things, make the first move, etc. I know that it doesn't mean I can't be these things if I thought of myself as the girl, but I guess I'm too worried about controlling where I fall within a relationship with another man."

"It often comes up and most people in my life joke about it. Sometimes it's a balance of both, but other times it does come down to stereotypical traits and what society has shown gender roles are. At the end of the day, it doesn't really bother me that I'm often labeled the girl, but I do think in reality, we're a mix of both. I like to be taken care of and protected, but I make more money and pay for more things. I know how to pitch a tent, but he will pump my gas."

"In my past seven-year relationship/marriage, some would say I was the 'girl,' wanting to be protected and taken care of, and I cast my ex-husband in the role of 'boy,' protector, etc. It's all true and it led to the dissolution of the marriage. Except I wouldn't slice it according to the boy/girl divide. I characterize it as me being the 'child' and him the 'parent.'"

"It's a balance. We switch off. Some days I need attention. Some days they do. I think a healthy relationship switches the archetypal traits of 'male' vs. 'female.'"

So that's what people gave me.

Having read all the responses to my question, I'm not sure I understand any better, but at least I know that I'm not the only one who finds the issue complicated and difficult to grapple with. I realize that I, too, go back and forth. There are times I feel like the boy as well; whenever anything technological in the house stops working, for example, or whenever there are forms to fill out. But in the matter of our wedding, evidently, I want Mike to be the boy.

Except now instead of Mike I want to marry the guy who said he felt like a garden gnome.

HGTV Urban Oasis Giveaway cards left to fill out: 4,786.

HGTV Urban Oasis Giveaway envelopes left to address: 4,800.

Friday, September 17

"Do you think if I asked really, really nicely," I said to Mike, "people in the neighborhood would stop handing me flyers to vote, in the upcoming Congressional election, for a candidate who believes in 'the Judeo-Christian tradition of marriage?'"

"No."

HGTV Urban Oasis Giveaway cards left to fill out: 4,765.

HGTV Urban Oasis Giveaway envelopes left to address: 4,800.

Saturday, September 18

I spent the day at the library, where I figured—accurately, as it happens—that nobody would be handing out flyers about the Judeo-Christian tradition of marriage, in an attempt to discover what the Judeo-Christian tradition of marriage actually is. And let me tell you, those politicians are way off the mark.

"Mike," I said when I got home, "guess what I learned today."

"To obey me?"

"Funny. No, I learned that there's a good reason I've always hated the term 'Judeo-Christian.'"

"It would have been better if you'd learned to obey me. But go ahead. What's the reason?"

"Well, you know how I'm like, Christians are the only people who ever say 'Judeo-Christian' and it's really just another word for Christian?" (Seriously: have you *ever* heard a Jew use the term

"Judeo-Christian" other than Dennis Prager, radio host and embarrassment to Judaism?)

"Yeah."

"That's because it's *always* been just another word for Christian."

The term first came into the vernacular, it turns out, with the rise of Hitler to the east; American Nazi supporters kept forming groups with names like the Christian American Crusade and the Christian Aryan Syndicate and publishing periodicals like *The Christian Defender*, so if the good guys wanted to make it clear that they weren't German sympathizers they had to use something else, and lo and behold! "Judeo-Christian" was born as a way to say "we're Christian and we think Nazis are bad." After the war, however, even though the Nazis were gone, Christians couldn't go back to "the Christian tradition" without implying that they thought Hitler had had the right idea, so "Judeo-Christian" stuck, which was lucky, because almost immediately people needed a term that meant "we think Communists are bad," and "Judeo-Christian" served nicely. Then, around the time same-sexers started pointing out that the Constitution applied to us, too, the Cold War ended, leaving "Judeo-Christian" free to become "we think gay people are bad"; after September 11, 2001, the term stretched to cover Muslims as well—nothing like a good twofer—which gets us to where we are today. "Judeo-Christian" is and always has been a term used by the majority to mean "us— and, more importantly, not them."

The problem is that the term "Judeo-Christian" *doesn't make any sense.*

The reasoning employed by those who call anything "Judeo-Christian" goes, as far as I can tell, something like this: The Jews have the Old Testament. Jesus just added a bunch of stuff and made a few edits to what was already there, so really Christianity is Judaism plus the New Testament. The only difference between Jews and Christians is that Jews don't believe the messiah has come yet, while Christians believe Jesus was the messiah (which in itself seems to be about as logical as saying that the only difference between war and peace is that war has a lot of people shooting each other with guns, but nobody asked me).

The problem with this view is that the Old Testament, which Jews call the written Torah, is only half the law. (I didn't need the library for this; I remembered from Sunday school—really, guys, you should give Mrs. Grossman a raise.) It's linked inextricably to the oral Torah, which is essentially the instruction manual for the written Torah. When Moses was up on Sinai, after he'd taken all that dictation, God said, okay, so those are the rules, now I need to explain how they work. And Moses was like, um, Buddy, I've already developed a repetitive stress injury from writing this down, and I still have those rocks with commandments carved into them to carry back with me, how about I just take a breather and listen really carefully and promise to remember? So he did, and when his meeting with God was finished Moses explained the instructions to all the guys he'd picked to run things once he was gone, and they all told their kids, and they all told their kids, and so on and so forth, until the Romans destroyed the Holy Temple in 70 A.D. (as a Jew I ought to say C.E., since as far as I'm concerned I'm not living in the year of anybody's lord, but I recognize that one has to make compromises) and with it what was left of the Jewish nation.

The deracinated Jews began to scatter all over the world, and as they did so they figured that, since there was no longer a group of people whose job it was to keep track, it might not be a bad idea to start writing this stuff down. A century or two later somebody collected everything he could get his hands on and wrote a sort of Cliffs Notes to the oral Torah called the Mishnah (which later on got its own Cliffs Notes, called the Talmud). The problem was that by this time Rabbi Yochanan, living in Yavne, had written one thing, while Rabbi Akiva in Bene Berak had written another, and Rabbi Tarphon in Lod yet another, either because they remembered things differently or because they figured the instruction manual could do with a little updating, and there was nobody to say which of them was right, so the Mishnah and the Talmud had to include all of them. In this way, these texts are kind of like the anti-Pope. When the Pope speaks *ex cathedra* in the Vatican, that's the truth, the whole truth, and nothing but the truth, forever and ever, or at least for a century or two until the Church is shamed into recanting it. In the Talmud, when anybody says anything under any circumstances, sure, what the hell, the more the merrier, that's true too.

This is all a very idyllic view of the matter, to be sure. Yes, for many Jews the question is often more important in theory than the answer, but nowadays that doesn't stop crazy people from feuding viciously with other crazy people because one of them used the wrong knife to kill a chicken. But if we're talking about the Judeo-Christian *tradition*—or, we might as well say, the Judaic tradition—then I see no reason not to go by what we think it used to be rather than what it happens to be today. Why shouldn't we be able to Norman Rockwellize our past just as delusionally as the goyim?

"So what I'm thinking," I said to Mike, having explained all this, "is that, if 'Judaic tradition' means something completely different from 'Judeo-Christian tradition,' maybe the 'Judaic tradition of marriage' means something completely different from the 'Judeo-Christian tradition of marriage.'"

"Maybe it means that you have to obey me."

HGTV Urban Oasis Giveaway cards left to fill out: 4,765.

HGTV Urban Oasis Giveaway envelopes left to address: 4,800.

Sunday, September 19

The answer, I was not surprised to learn after another day at the library, is yes, the Judaic tradition of marriage means something very, very different. Very, very, *very* different.

Divorce and remarriage, for example, have always been part of the Jewish marital tradition (in contrast to Jesus, who said, "Whosoever shall put away his wife and marry another committeth adultery against her, and if a woman shall put away her husband, and be married to another, she committeth adultery," I'm looking at you, Newt Gingrich). The Talmudic divorce laws are, unfortunately, pretty sexist, but there are also some surprising exceptions. On the one hand, only a man can initiate a divorce, which suggests that an unhappy wife has little recourse. On the other hand, the ketubah is a serious matter: If a man divorces his wife and it's her first marriage, he has to pay her, depending on the authority you consult, either a) enough money to buy a minimum of a hundred goats, b) enough money for the *interest* to buy a minimum of a hundred goats a year, or c) enough money for the interest to support her for the rest of her life. Subsequent marriages have the same rules but it's only fifty goats instead of a hundred. (I must point out that the goat is my unit of measurement, not the Talmud's. The actual sum involved is two hundred zuzim, but it's been centuries since anybody knew how much a zuz was worth, so I went by the traditional Passover song about a child whose father buys a goat for two zuzim. According to this reckoning, two hundred zuzim would buy a hundred goats. A goat these days will run you somewhere between $100 and $350, which means the ketubah was worth up to $70,000, but that would be in B.C. dollars, which don't exist; the best I can do is to say that $70,000 in 1800 A.D. would be worth $885,710.32 today, but the calculation is artificial enough that I'd rather just stick with the goats.)

Furthermore, even if her husband doesn't want to divorce her, a woman who wants to leave him can sue to have the court force him to do so, and there were at least some periods during Jewish history during which she pretty much automatically won. If the court finds in favor of the wife and the husband refuses to divorce her, he's beaten until he consents. The list of reasons a woman can sue for divorce is extensive and includes things like providing her clothing inappropriate for her age, and, stunningly, failing to meet his sexual obligations to her.

The sages make this very clear: sexual pleasure is the woman's right and the man's obligation. Different frequencies are required depending on the man's occupation, so that a man of independent means, for example, has to offer his wife sex *every day* (though if he has several wives he just has to rotate through them daily); the Mishnah goes on to tell us that the frequency with which other men must offer their wives sex is, "for laborers, twice a week; for ass-drivers, once a week; for camel-drivers, once in thirty days; for sailors, once in six months. These are the rulings of Rabbi Eliezer." A man has a duty to make sure his wife enjoys sex; he also has to keep an eye out for indications that she's in the mood and offer it to her without her having to ask for it.

More succinctly put, the Talmud says that a man has to have sex with his wife on demand or she can divorce him and take him for a whole lot of goats.

Now I know why I think of myself as the girl.

Adultery, on the other hand, unlike divorce and women's sexual pleasure, is an issue on which we're in perfect agreement with Christians; after all, it says it right there in the ninth Commandment, Exodus 20:14: "Thou shalt not commit adultery." If a woman commits adultery her husband can either divorce her (paying her the appropriate number of goats) or sue her. If he sues her and she's found guilty, she's stoned to death, unless she's the daughter of a priest, in which case she's burned alive; either way, the man with whom she committed adultery magically dies at the same time. The Talmud is vague on the mechanics of this, but I find myself hoping that it's just like the Skeksis and the Mystics in *The Dark Crystal*, and wherever he is he's just suddenly pummeled to death with invisible rocks or he spontaneously combusts (I should note that my friend the Orthodox gay ex-rabbi calligrapher says he doesn't remember this, but it came from a source that was full of other stuff he said was on the money, so I stand by it). If the woman is found innocent, her husband is flogged and has to pay her two years' worth of a skilled laborer's salary.

(All of this is theoretical, by the way; after the temple was destroyed there were no priests and therefore no priests' daughters to burn alive.)

According to the Talmud if the man is married, and the woman is single, then it's not adultery. A man can have as many wives as he desires, although with a mind to his obligation to give each one sexual pleasure (remember, he rotates through the list) rabbis recommend four as a practical upper limit, so that no wife goes too long without the opportunity for sex. Premarital sex, although the rabbis frowned on it from a societal point of view, is actually fine as far as God is concerned.

Judaism tends to be pretty sex-positive in general; the Vilna Gaon says that one ought to get an erection while studying Torah, and the eighteenth-century founder of Hasidic Judaism explains that the reason Jews rock back and forth while praying is that prayer is sex with the feminine aspect of God.

Whoops. Mike's home. Time to argue about what proportion of the cupcakes for the reception will be chocolate. I myself don't see the need for more than two or three non-chocolate cupcakes, but Mike has promised me a persuasive argument for a one-third chocolate, one-third lemon, and one-third red velvet split.

No ketubah yet, but it turns out that, according to the Talmud, a ketubah written on the horn of a cow is valid, so we may have more options than I realized.

HGTV Urban Oasis Giveaway cards left to fill out: 4,765.

HGTV Urban Oasis Giveaway envelopes left to address: 4,800.

Monday, September 20

Prostitution—this has to be the last day I spend at the library, because it's really cutting into my HGTV-Urban-Oasis-Giveaway-card-filling-out time—is technically against the rules. However, the Talmud tells some interesting stories about rabbis who, as they traveled from city to city, would send ahead a week or so before their arrival so that when they got to town they could ask, "Who will be my wife for the night?" The town would produce a suitable woman (it's unclear to me whether she had any say in the matter), the rabbi would marry her, they would spend the night doing the sorts of things one imagines they might do, and then the next day they would divorce, at which point the town would pay her the divorce settlement of a hundred goats (and she would be free to marry again if she liked). Which seems like a high price to pay even for a night of unimaginable ecstasy, but hey, I paid $12.50 to see *Season of the Witch*, so who am I to talk?

The Talmud doesn't love jacking off. Here's one place where the goyim have it easier than we do, at least as far as men go. Judaism takes very seriously God's command to "be fruitful and multiply," and, while few sages go so far as to forbid masturbation entirely, nobody's particularly fond of the idea of spilling seed. (Rabbi Ishmael commands, "Thou shalt not practice masturbation either with hand or with foot"; when I got back from the library this afternoon I spent twenty minutes trying to maneuver myself into a position from which I could masturbate with my foot. When I finally managed it, I was good for about ten seconds before feeling spasms of excruciating pain in some leg muscle I didn't know I had, so all I can say is that Rabbi Ishmael must have been one flexible bastard. Luckily my failure did not impede my ability to write the cards for the HGTV Urban Oasis Giveaway.) Here again the law is mute when it comes to women, so apparently they're free to masturbate to their hearts' content.

Anal and oral sex are both fine. "Meat which comes from the slaughterhouse," points out one rabbi when asked about this, "may be eaten salted, roasted, cooked, or boiled; so with fish from the fishmonger." And what about the fact that a male orgasm during anal or oral sex spills seed nonprocreatively? Apparently this isn't a problem "unless it is his intention to destroy the seed and it is his habit always to do so. However, if it is occasional and the desire of his heart is to come upon his wife in an unnatural way [i.e., anally or orally], it is permitted."

When it comes to abortion—not that Mike and I are likely to have to confront the question, but what the hell, it was only a few more pages of reading—for the first forty days a fetus is "considered to be mere water," and the majority opinion seems to be therefore that abortion during that time is no problem. After that, the fetus is alive, but still most certainly not a person, and its life is absolutely less important than its mother's. Though there were some conservatives who dissented, most rabbis agreed that the moment at which it becomes a human being is when it has come halfway out of its mother's body; others went further still and argued that a newborn isn't human until its thirteenth day. I don't suppose they allowed infanticide if a baby was born and a week later you decided you didn't want it, but there it is.

On the question of homosexuality the Talmud is, alas, less enlightened than one would wish; anal sex between two men is forbidden (though now that I think about it I didn't find anything on the books prohibiting anal sex when you're talking about *more than* two men, so maybe orgies and double penetration are exempt). The sages are silent, however, about any other kind of gay male sex, and, though what little they say about lesbian sex is disapproving, it's extraordinarily half-hearted. So the Judaic part of the Judeo-Christian tradition allows guys to suck each other's cocks till the cows come home, and women can do whatever they want with each other as long as they don't mind the occasional finger being wagged at them.

(Furthermore, for the Biblically prescribed punishment to be carried out, there have to be two witnesses. There's a great story in the Talmud about a rabbi who catches two guys screwing. He says, wait, you're screwing, you're not allowed to do that. And they say, "Yes, but you are one, and we are two.")

One of the best books I found was by Steven Greenberg, the first openly gay Orthodox rabbi. Called *Wrestling with God and Man: Homosexuality in the Jewish Tradition*, it proposes a new interpretation of the Biblical passages we've read heretofore as forbidding gay anal sex; Greenberg suggests, compellingly, a reading of the text that leaves sexual orientation and position alone and forbids any intercourse, gay or straight, whose purpose is to degrade or humiliate (which I suppose might be unhappy news to S/M fetishists but my guess is that they're not too concerned with the Talmudic correctness of what they're up to). He acknowledges that this gay-friendly interpretation flies in the face of thousands of years of Jewish tradition—except I suspect he would probably also say that it's completely in line with thousands of years of Jewish tradition, which is all about arguing, reinterpreting, and continually rediscovering the meaning of a living text.

"So what you're telling me," said Mike after I shared what I had learned with him, "is that the Judeo-Christian tradition of marriage actually includes divorce, polygamy, prostitution, abortion, and gay oral sex?"

"And gay orgies and double penetration. Don't forget the gay orgies and double penetration."

"Somebody better tell Rick Santorum."

HGTV Urban Oasis Giveaway cards left to fill out: 4,621.

HGTV Urban Oasis Giveaway envelopes left to address: 4,700.

Tuesday, September 21

Yesterday my stepmother (who when I'd mentioned early on that I had no idea what kind of a wedding I wanted or how many people I wanted to invite looked at me as if I'd just eaten a baby) asked me where we were registered, and I told her about my plan to have a friend email everybody and tell them to donate to charity.

"No," said my stepmother.

"What do you mean, no? You were supposed to say, how selfless of you."

"I mean, no. It's fine to tell people to give money to charity, but you also have to register somewhere, because if people *want* to give you a real gift, it's inconsiderate not to let them."

So, after she remained unswayed despite all my efforts, Mike and I have registered at Z Gallerie, which is the gayest store on the face of the earth.

It is one of the world's great tragedies that the physical Z Gallerie store in New York is no longer open, because when Mike and I needed a vacation but couldn't actually take one it used to be almost enough to go there and spend a few hours wandering among their collection of gewgaws, statuary, art, glass, and cute kitchen paraphernalia. Sconces made out of iron, sconces made out of silver, sconces made out of pewter, sconces made out of wood. Art deco end tables. And kitschy stuff, but classy kitsch, like black bat sunglasses for Hallowe'en that actually make you look sexy, or silver moose salt and pepper shakers. At least half of their wares involve either mirrors or feathers or both. Z Gallerie was where Mike got the purple star Christmas tree ornament that started this whole thing in the first place. Really, the best way I can think of to describe Z Gallerie is to say that it sells Gay Stuff. You walk in and you're breathing gay dust.

So here are some of the things we've registered for (following the principle that there should be gifts at all price ranges, for guests at all income levels):

Scented candles (Sandalwood, Tuscan Blood, Madagascar Spice, Bali Lime Papaya, Egyptian Bergamot, Tunisian Jasmine).

A set of glasses whose rims are cut on the diagonal.

A set of copper napkin rings cast to look like pheasants, with feathers attached.

(See? Gay, gay, gay.)

Terracotta placemats.

Mirrored sconces.

Sconces with feathers.

Mirrored sconces with feathers.

Various vases, lamps, and tables united only by their utter gayness.

A copper fountain for the garden. A coffee table that looks like a seventeenth-century expedition trunk. An art deco chaise longue. Carved panels for the wall.

Something that has a mirror and feathers on it and I don't even know what it's for but it's gorgeous.

WE'RE SO GAY.

Meanwhile, I have asked Sarah (my accomplice on the reality show) to send the following email to all the people we've invited.

Dear Potential Guest at Mike and Joel's Wedding,

I hope you're as excited as I am that Mike and Joel are finally tying the knot. I'm writing because I just had a conversation with them that seems worth mentioning to other guests.

What Mike and Joel want most for their wedding is for us all to be there to share the occasion with them, but for those of us interested in celebrating with a gift, they're hoping we'll make donations in their honor to Doctors Without Borders, Freedom to Marry, or another charity important to us. If you can't bear to mark the event without a physical gift, they're registered at Z Gallerie, but they would be happy with anything it pleased you to give them.

Sincerely yours,

Sarah

It's too bad Z Gallerie doesn't carry Karl Rove's head.

Of course, they could always get a shipment in next week. Then they could cover it in mirrors and feathers and sell it to us.

HGTV Urban Oasis Giveaway cards left to fill out: 4,591.

HGTV Urban Oasis Giveaway envelopes left to address: 4,628.

Wednesday, September 22

And now I wish to God we had been slightly less gay and registered, like normal people, at Sears or something, because our dishwasher broke yesterday, and when the plumber came out to take a look at it he told us we had to replace it. I have therefore moved the portable dishwasher up from the basement so that our dishes can still get clean while we look for a new one.

Mike and I bought this house from the daughters of the ninety-year-old man who had been living in it for fifty years, the last twenty alone after his wife died. When we moved in, the kitchen was an empty box containing literally nothing but a small refrigerator and a beat-up sink, so changing that was high on our list of priorities. I found some cabinetry on Craigslist, and Mike called a plumber about installing appliances. "The sink can go there," Mike said when we were making plans, "and the stove can go there."

"What about the dishwasher?" I said.

"What do you mean? We're not getting a dishwasher."

"Um, yes, we are." We had never lived together before, and though we had talked about a lot of the conflicts we might face this was not a problem we had foreseen.

"No, we're not. I've never had a dishwasher, and I wouldn't use one if we got it."

"You think having a dishwasher is a sign of moral weakness, don't you?" I said.

"Honey, of *course* having a dishwasher is a sign of moral weakness," he replied. "You're the one who's deluding yourself by saying it's not."

So the next day, without consulting Mike, I went out and bought a portable dishwasher off Craigslist, which enraged him when he found out what I'd done, and then that night I cooked dinner using every single container in the kitchen.

The problem, we realized gradually, was that I had grown up in a home where the person who cooked the food was exempt from doing the dishes, while Mike had grown up in a home where the person who cooked the food also did the dishes (usually this person was him). So when he cooks, he uses one bowl or pot or pan and cleans up as he goes and after dinner there are exactly three things to be cleaned: the bowl or pot or pan he cooked the food in, the utensils he made and ate it with, and the plates he ate it from. Whereas when I cook, the list of things that need to be cleaned swells by, for an average dinner, another two bowls, three pots, five pans, six knives, the garlic press, the colander, the Cuisinart, the blender, the counter, the floor, and occasionally the ceiling. (You can see how I would be inconvenienced by the disappearance of the pot and pan lids I put in the basement when I was mad at Mike, which are STILL MISSING, by the way.) So for the first several months of our cohabitation, I would create these extravagant messes in the kitchen and then not clean them up, because that was Mike's job, while Mike sat and simmered in growing resentment and didn't clean them up, because it was my job. "Every time you called me and told me you'd baked me a pie," he later told me, "I was filled with dread of what I was going to come home and see in the kitchen."

Eventually I persuaded Mike to install an actual dishwasher, putting the portable one in the basement; over time we've both managed to move toward the middle, and these days the cooking and the cleaning up both migrate vaguely between us. But it's too bad Z Gallerie doesn't have a mirror-and-feather-covered dishwasher, because this battered old portable thing isn't going to last long.

HGTV Urban Oasis Giveaway cards left to fill out: 4,409.

HGTV Urban Oasis Giveaway envelopes left to address: 4,572.

Thursday, September 23

Today is the day I had to send the travel agent the balance of the honeymoon payment, but, inexplicably, no publisher called me at the last minute to offer me a huge advance for my next book, and no producer called me at the last minute to offer me a huge advance for my next show, even though I was *totally* ready for the money to appear, so the only way I was able to pay for the honeymoon was to steal one of Mike's checks, forge his signature, and deposit it in my account.

The way I see it, I'm still technically paying for the honeymoon. I mean, it was my account number I gave the travel agent over the phone, after all.

And I'll totally pay Mike back, some day, probably, though once we're happily ensconced in our urban oasis I'm sure he won't even notice the money is missing.

HGTV Urban Oasis Giveaway cards left to fill out: 4,270.

HGTV Urban Oasis Giveaway envelopes left to address: 4,363.

Friday, September 24

Here is how my conversation with the guy in the formalwear store yesterday began.

```
                                        FADE IN:

     INT. A FORMALWEAR STORE--DAY

     Mike and Joel enter, thrumming with excite-
     ment about their impending nuptials.

     As Guy in the Formalwear Store comes obsequi-
     ously up to him:

                     JOEL
          Hi, I called earlier. My fiancé and I
          are here to be fitted for morning
          clothes.

                     GUY IN THE FORMALWEAR STORE
          Oh, yes. Step this way and let me take
          your measurements.

                     MIKE
          Please don't tell us what the numbers
          are.

                     GUY IN THE FORMALWEAR STORE
          There are no numbers in this store.

                     JOEL
          We love you.
```

Here is how it continued in my fantasy world:

            GUY IN THE FORMALWEAR STORE
All right, here are your sets of
morning clothes, each complete with
top hat, dove gray waistcoat, dashing
ascot, shoes, and lemon gloves.

            JOEL
         (as they exit)
Thank you so much!

                   FADE TO BLACK.

Here, alas, is how it actually continued:

            GUY IN THE FORMALWEAR STORE
          (indicating dummy with set
         of morning clothes on it)
All right, so we'll get together sets
of morning clothes for both of you
with the options you requested, using
this combination as a base.

            JOEL
Great! I see the waistcoat is just a
false front, though; I'd love an
actual waistcoat.

            GUY IN THE FORMALWEAR STORE
Why? You'll just sweat through the
whole ceremony.

            JOEL
You're probably right, but I'd still
love an actual waistcoat.

                    GUY IN THE FORMALWEAR STORE
          Well, we don't have any.

                    JOEL
                         (after a pause)
          Hmm. Maybe I can just wear one of the
          ones I have at home.

                    MIKE
          Sweetheart, I'm not sure any of those
          still fit you.

                    JOEL
          Shut up.
                         (to Guy in the Formalwear
                         Store)
          Okay. How about a top hat?

                    GUY IN THE FORMALWEAR STORE
          Gee, we don't have many of those.

                    JOEL
                         (under his breath)
          But you're a *formalwear store*.

                    GUY IN THE FORMALWEAR STORE
          Let me go check in the back and see
          what's in stock.

          He leaves. He returns with a gray top hat.

                    GUY IN THE FORMALWEAR STORE
          This is the only one we have, and I
          think it's probably too big for you.

                    JOEL
        Why don't I try it on, just to see?

He tries the hat on. It engulfs him.

                    GUY IN THE FORMALWEAR STORE
        Yeah, that's what I thought.

                    JOEL
        You're sure there are no more back
        there?

                    GUY IN THE FORMALWEAR STORE
        There are, but they're black.

                    JOEL
        Oh, great! Could you take a look,
        please?

                    GUY IN THE FORMALWEAR STORE
        You can't wear a black top hat with
        morning clothes at a wedding. Only
        gray.

                    JOEL
        Actually, that's a myth that sprang
        up when they stopped manufacturing
        silk plush after the last looms used
        to weave it were destroyed in the
        owner's bitter feud with his brother,
        who--

Guy in the Formalwear Store exits mid-sentence.
He returns with two black top hats.

                Taking Care of Last-Minute Details   195

                    JOEL
          Oh, thanks!

He tries one of the hats on. It fits. Mike tries
the other hat on. It also fits.

                    GUY IN THE FORMALWEAR STORE
          This just looks so wrong to me.

                    JOEL
          No, I promise, the gray top hat thing
          really is a myth, it--

                    GUY IN THE FORMALWEAR STORE
          I know what it's supposed to look like.

                    JOEL
                    (to Mike, under his breath)
          Is there a copy of <u>Modern Bride</u> I can
          hit this guy with?
                    (to Guy in the formalwear
                    store)
          Well, I appreciate your patience with
          us. If I ask for an ascot, it'll be real,
          right? Not a clip-on?

                    GUY IN THE FORMALWEAR STORE
          Yes, it'll be real.

                    JOEL
          That's terrific. Now, about the
          gloves--

                    MIKE
          Joel, I really don't want to wear
          gloves. Can we leave?

                    GUY IN THE FORMALWEAR STORE
Come and pick these up the day before
the wedding.

                    JOEL
Thank you.

                    GUY IN THE FORMALWEAR STORE
It still looks wrong.

                    JOEL
No, really, they--

                    MIKE
Honey.

                    JOEL
Thank you.
          (under his breath as they
          leave)
It's a myth.

                              FADE TO BLACK.

HGTV Urban Oasis Giveaway cards left to fill out: 4,026.
HGTV Urban Oasis Giveaway envelopes left to address: 4,188.

Saturday, September 25

I went by the Brooklyn Botanic Garden today to fill out some
paperwork. It had spaces for "Bride" and "Groom."
   "You folks need to fix this," I said.
   "Tell me about it," said the obviously lesbian woman (blue
spiky hair, three nose rings, "Dykes Rule!" button) behind the
counter.

So I crossed out "Bride" and wrote in "Groom." And I laughed at how an entire architecture of prejudice could be toppled with the stroke of a pen.

HGTV Urban Oasis Giveaway cards left to fill out: 3,865.

HGTV Urban Oasis Giveaway envelopes left to address: 4,012.

Sunday, September 26

"You should talk about our wedding as part of the fight against injustice," I said to Rachel, "but it can't be just about fighting marriage inequality or even fighting discrimination against same-sexers. That's not enough. Injustice in the world reaches so much farther and so much deeper than that. If people leave the wedding thinking only about trying to make the world better for same-sexers then I feel like we'll have failed. They need to be thinking about trying to make the world better for *everybody* who's oppressed, in any way, anywhere."

"Got it," she said. "Do you have a ketubah yet?"

HGTV Urban Oasis Giveaway cards left to fill out: 3,644.

HGTV Urban Oasis Giveaway envelopes left to address: 4,012.

Monday, September 27

WE HAVE A KETUBAH! And it's purple! I have no idea what led Mike to approve it even though it's such an extravagant color; I think it was at least in part that it looks Artistic. But I don't care, because at last I can stop worrying about the damn thing.

HGTV Urban Oasis Giveaway cards left to fill out: 3,453.

HGTV Urban Oasis Giveaway envelopes left to address: 3,978.

Tuesday, September 28

Yesterday we received an RSVP in the mail from Mike's cousins (who we already knew wouldn't be able to come). It read something like this:

Dear Mike and Joel,

Thank you for the invitation to your wedding. Since we're Catholic and follow the Church's teaching, we can't accept, but we send you all our love and hope that the day is a wonderful one.

Love,
George and Frances

At first when I read this I was just nonplussed. I mean, it's 2010; who sends an RSVP like that in 2010?

But as the day wore on, I started to get angry. First of all, the correct way to decline an invitation is, "George and Frances regret that they will be unable to accept the very kind invitation of Joel Derfner and Michael Combs on Sunday, the tenth of October." Note that doing so involves no mention of why George and Frances are declining or what they might or might not believe about the wedding and its validity.

I showed the note to Mike when he got home. "Look, Joel," he said, "Frances is the one who talks about everybody in the family behind their backs."

"Maybe she didn't understand what she was doing."

"She understood exactly what she was doing. Remember, she read your last book and then called everybody she could think of to talk about how scandalous it was that I was dating a stripper."

"She did *what*?"

"Whoops. I thought I told you that."

"But she was so *nice* to me when I met her."

"That's Frances for you. I'm sure she was drunk when she wrote this, anyway. Just let it go."

But I couldn't let it go. I grew angrier and angrier, and when we went to bed I lay awake, tossing and turning. Finally I had an idea, got up, did some Googling, and found that an organization such as I had in mind did indeed exist. This allowed me to write (on handmade Nepalese paper, no less) and send the following letter today:

Dear George and Frances,

Thank you so much for your kind note; of course we understand why you can't attend. We felt our wedding wouldn't be a true celebration, however, without having you involved in some way, so we made donations in your honor to Freedom to Marry and to SNAP, the Survivors' Network of those Abused by Priests.

We hope you're well and we look forward to seeing you some time soon.

Love,
Joel and Mike

(Sometimes even I am impressed by my evil genius.)

When I told Mike about the response I'd written, he laughed and said, "You should send it. It would serve her right."

"Oh, I already did."

"Please tell me you're joking."

"Okay, I'm joking."

"You're not joking, are you?"

"No."

Let this be a lesson, by the by, that etiquette is neither "stupid rules about which fork to use" nor "just about making people feel comfortable," both of which descriptions I have seen offered as definitions. Dinnerware and social lubrication do indeed find themselves under the umbrella of etiquette, but they are joined there by techniques for smiling sweetly at your adversaries as you cut their hearts out.

HGTV Urban Oasis Giveaway cards left to fill out: 3,322.

HGTV Urban Oasis Giveaway envelopes left to address: 3,867.

Wednesday, September 29

We forgot to buy rings.

HGTV Urban Oasis Giveaway cards left to fill out: 3,235.

HGTV Urban Oasis Giveaway envelopes left to address: 3,745.

Thursday, September 30

The Department of Justice is visiting Mike's hospital—I think this has something to do with the woman who showed up in the emergency room, waited for twenty-five hours to be seen, and died, though I must point out that this happened a full three weeks before Mike started working there; eventually they named a conference room after her, which makes me angry, because I think she should have gotten at least a wing if not an entire building—so I've volunteered to take care of the rings.

I have determined that, given the postage for the HGTV Urban Oasis Giveaway, along with the portion of my own money I have left to spend on the honeymoon, my budget for wedding rings is twenty dollars. I would just steal more money from Mike, but I think he's discovered the earlier theft, because he's moved his checkbook to somewhere I can't find it.

HGTV Urban Oasis Giveaway cards left to fill out: 3,178.

HGTV Urban Oasis Giveaway envelopes left to address: 3,745.

Friday, October 1

I am making very little headway on the HGTV Urban Oasis Giveaway entries. I have done the calculations and if I allocate eight hours per day to sleep and an hour and a half to meals and hygiene, then to get them all done in time I have to fill out roughly one card or envelope every waking minute.

This is not going to happen.

So I posted an ad on Craigslist a few hours ago, under the heading $50 TO HELP ME WITH TEDIOUS TASK ON SUNDAY. I couldn't decide which category to put it in, so after considering Labor and Event I finally went with Writing, figuring that sometimes it's okay to be exceedingly literal. I wrote a funny paragraph describing the situation and then said, "The only requirements are that you have decent handwriting and that you be entertaining, because if I'm going to spend four hours with you doing a task this boring I want the conversation to take my mind off the soul-numbing tedium."

I've received a number of responses so far, but only a few from people who were even mildly amusing, so I've contacted them, along with one who wasn't particularly amusing but whose email signature was the URL for his profile on modelmayhem.com. I took a look and wrote him back immediately, forbearing to tell him that I would double his pay if he did the gig shirtless or that I was open to more involved arrangements as well.

HGTV Urban Oasis Giveaway cards left to fill out: 3,078.

HGTV Urban Oasis Giveaway envelopes left to address: 3,745.

Saturday, October 2

It looks as if I'll have four or five people to help me tomorrow (depending on whether I ask the model to fill out cards and envelopes or just sit or stand, godlike, off to the side).

HGTV Urban Oasis Giveaway cards left to fill out: 3,078.

HGTV Urban Oasis Giveaway envelopes left to address: 3,745.

Sunday, October 3

God hates me and does not want me to win an apartment in Manhattan. None of the Craigslist people I emailed with showed up. I'm trying to figure out how to continue communicating with the model without being stalkerish, but so far I'm coming up empty.

HGTV Urban Oasis Giveaway cards left to fill out: Never mind.

HGTV Urban Oasis Giveaway envelopes left to address: Fuck you, HGTV.

Monday, October 4

From: Joel Derfner
To: Mike Combs
Time: 11:26 a.m.

Honey, I found some rings. Take a look at this URL. We can replace them after the wedding, but at least they'll do for now.

From: Mike Combs
To: Joel Derfner
Time: 1:13 p.m.

At $7.99 apiece, what could go wrong?

~~HGTV Urban Oasis Giveaway cards left to fill out:~~
~~HGTV Urban Oasis Giveaway envelopes left to address:~~

Tuesday, October 5

"Honey, great news!" I said this evening. "I was just talking to a photographer friend of mine and she's willing to shoot the wedding for a huge discount! We don't have to go out and buy little disposable Kodak cameras for all our guests and have the photos they take be the only photos of our wedding after all!"

This was a lie. The photographer quoted me her standard rate, which on top of the sixteen dollars for wedding rings is money I don't even come close to having, but the thought of throwing Kodak mini-cameras at our guests—a plan Mike actually argued for—and ending up with a bunch of photographs of us seen through a delicate haze of cupcake icing is too much for me to bear.

~~HGTV Urban Oasis Giveaway cards left to fill out:~~
~~HGTV Urban Oasis Giveaway envelopes left to address:~~

Wednesday, October 6

I emailed a bunch of my students and told them that if they came over and helped me with the Urban Oasis Giveaway cards and envelopes I would feed them pizza and beer. Several of them showed up and made short work of the afternoon, and I am much closer to my goal of moving back to Manhattan.

HGTV Urban Oasis Giveaway cards left to fill out: 1,837.

HGTV Urban Oasis Giveaway envelopes left to address: 2,044.

Thursday, October 7

I just got back from Home Depot—I almost called Mike to tell him that I was there of my own volition—where I did the butchest thing I've ever done in my entire life, which was *use a saw to cut pieces of wood to make poles for the chuppah.*

Then I spent twenty minutes trying to decide whether or not to paint them mulberry, which brought the butch factor right back down into the negatives again, but still, it was an exhilarating moment.

HGTV Urban Oasis Giveaway cards left to fill out: 1,523.

HGTV Urban Oasis Giveaway envelopes left to address: 1,809.

Friday, October 8

"There's all this *God*," I wailed to Rachel on the phone today after reading the outline of the ceremony she'd sent me along with the texts to be recited in various places.

"Well, you said you wanted a traditional Jewish ceremony."

"Yeah, but not one with *God* in it. God doesn't *exist*. The universe is a cruel, caliginous, uncaring wasteland. I don't want my wedding to be full of a lie. We have to start over."

"Joel, the ceremony is in two days. We're not starting over. But let me take a look at what we've got and see what I can come up with. Where it says, 'in the name of God,' I can definitely substitute 'in the name of love.' Would that be a good start?"

"Yes."

HGTV Urban Oasis Giveaway cards left to fill out: 1,369.

HGTV Urban Oasis Giveaway envelopes left to address: 1,487.

Saturday, October 9

I picked up the clothes from the formalwear store with three minutes to spare before they closed.

And I must have done something really, really bad in a past life, because the ascot is a clip-on.

I'm going to look like a mountebank at my own wedding. Tomorrow.

HGTV Urban Oasis Giveaway cards left to fill out: 1,024.

HGTV Urban Oasis Giveaway envelopes left to address: 1,245.

9

Getting Married

The thing that strikes me most is the silence.

I don't know whether Rachel has read Walter Kaufmann, whose thoughts on ritual helped me understand what I wanted out of a wedding ceremony, and wants us to hear "the voice that the rest of the time one is prone to forget," but I'm amazed at her ability to be silent. Mike and I, having circled each other seven times (it did get a little dizzying by the end), are standing in front of her under the chuppah and she's saying nothing.

The Brooklyn Botanic Garden is gorgeous, and the Japanese Hill and Pond Garden is the most gorgeous part of it. Jesus, it's so beautiful I almost feel silly.

Rachel is still silent, but it's a full silence, not an empty one.

Julia looks so beautiful in that dress. And Victoria's shoes are stunning. And I love the smile on Sarah's face. And Peter and Len and Sean

seem so dignified, and Angelo has never been hotter. And I hope Jason and April will be doing this soon themselves.

"Bruchim haba'im b'shem ahavah; Bruchot haba'ot b'shem ahavah," Rachel finally says. "Blessed are we who have gathered in the name of love." And then she goes back to being silent.

Oh, look, the koi have gathered here from around the pond! It's like the fish want to watch our wedding.

The thing about this silence is that it doesn't feel uncomfortable, like silence usually does, like when you've run out of things to say to somebody you don't know well. This silence really does feel like it's leaving room—no, creating room—for everybody to calm down, to settle, to relax. Rachel's silence somehow sanctifies the time and place, and we New Yorkers, constantly on alert, constantly on the lookout for the next crazy homeless person who's going to accost us on the subway or the next car that's almost going to hit us or the next piece of electronic equipment we're going to have to buy: in this moment, we feel safe. Our guard begins to drop. As the silence continues and nothing alarming happens, no alligator jumps out of the pond to eat us all, nobody makes a joke that requires a witty response, I feel the tension draining from my body—God, I sound like a meditation prompt, but I swear it's true—and my focus coming to rest here and now.

"Splendor is upon everything," Rachel finally says, giving a loose translation of the traditional blessing of the couple under the chuppah. "Blessing is upon everything. Everything full of this abundance, bless these loving grooms."

"The circles you have just walked," she says, "are a symbol that you have made each other central to your lives, set apart, holy, created sacred space that is yours alone to share. Now you stand under the chuppah, a symbol of the home you have created and will continue to create. It's open on all sides, welcoming, surrounded by loved ones. Yet the flimsiness of the chuppah reminds us that the only thing real about a home is the people in it who love each other and choose to be together, choose to be a family. The only anchor they will have to hold on to will be each other's hands. Joel and Mike, may your home be a place of abounding love, creativity, passion, and peace."

My dad and my aunt Suzie step forward to light the candle to commemorate the departed. (We're Jews. We can't pick up the mail without commemorating the departed.)

I wish my mom were here.

Rachel picks up the wine bottle.

"You can just use grape juice for the kiddush," she said last week when I told her I don't drink. The reason I don't drink is that I sang in my college's church choir, and as a chorister I was invited to the parties thrown with some regularity at the house of Peter Gomes, minister in the church and Plummer Professor of

Christian Morals. At these parties Professor Gomes served, among other refreshments, a concoction of his own invention called Bishop's Punch, which was made up of one part fruit juice to two parts bourbon. During the first few parties I acquitted myself admirably—and when I sang at Professor Gomes's piano a blood alcohol concentration of 0.19 did wonders for my Mendelssohn—but eventually, like Icarus flying toward the sun, I went too far and was hard put to explain my dry heaves during Introduction to Homeric Greek the next afternoon. Since then, the taste of alcohol has turned my stomach.

Grape juice struck me, therefore, as a more than satisfactory alternative, until I opened the refrigerator this morning and realized that we had forgotten to buy grape juice. The grocery store around the corner wasn't going to open till after we left for the Garden, which meant we were limited to whatever was in our kitchen. This proved after a few minutes' searching to be Diet Coke, Diet Mountain Dew, chicken broth, apple juice, slightly turned milk, water, appletini mixer (unlike me, Mike does tipple now and again), and High Efficiency Tide laundry detergent.

So apple juice it was; the problem now was what to put it in, because I would be damned if my wedding photographs were all going to feature prominently a 64-ounce plastic bottle of Juicy Juice. So I rooted through cabinets until I found an appropriately-sized Tupperware box, filled it half-full with apple juice, and then realized that a Tupperware box of ersatz wine would be even worse than a bottle of Juicy Juice. So I grabbed a bottle of Trader Joe's wine, uncorked it, poured it down the sink, transferred the apple juice from the Tupperware to the bottle, and went to get dressed.

"Wine," says Rachel now to the assembled guests, "is a symbol of joy and of celebration of life's energy. Mike and Joel, let this . . . um . . . apple juice—"

"Wine," I hiss.

"Let this wine represent the sweetness we wish for your married life. As you drink from it, we pray that the joys you share be doubled and any bitterness be halved."

We both take sips of apple juice.

"Mike and Joel are now going to exchange rings using words they have chosen."

My little first cousins once removed from Los Angeles step solemnly forward, holding out the ring boxes on which I'd used a Sharpie to scrawl "M" and "J." ("You've got to help me out here," their father, my first cousin, wrote me. "My kids won't shut up about wanting to know what they're doing in your wedding. Please, just give them something. Anything. They can hold a fucking flower. But you have to do something. Because this is going to kill me soon if you don't.")

"I am my beloved's," I say, quoting the Song of Solomon, as I put the ring on Mike's finger, "and my beloved is mine."

"I am my beloved," he says, putting the ring on my finger, "and my beloved is mine."

"I am my *beloved's*," I say under my breath, thinking, *I'm the narcissist in this relationship, buddy.*

"I am my beloved's, and my beloved is mine."

I am my beloved's, and my beloved is mine.

"A ketubah," says Rachel, "is a legal document that makes this marriage official within the Jewish community. Mike and Joel have chosen two witnesses who will come forward to read it. If they find all that it contains acceptable, they will sign their names, followed by Joel and Mike, and then me." My friend Sarah and Mike's friend Aaron come up to the tiny table we brought from the back yard to examine the ketubah, which is written in Hebrew, a language neither of them speaks. They nonetheless find it acceptable and sign their names, followed by me, Mike, and Rachel. I'm careful to make my signature neat, and I love the thick line the

Sharpie produces. "This ketubah," says Rachel, "has been witnessed and signed according to tradition. It is valid and binding. Mike and Joel will now read it aloud."

"I betroth you to me forever," Mike and I read in translated unison. Rachel said we could do it that way or alternating sentences; Mike wanted to alternate, but that seemed very second-grade to me, so I strategically turned the conversation to other matters so that when the moment came, since we hadn't practiced alternating and didn't know who'd start, we would pretty much have to read in unison. "I betroth you to me in everlasting faithfulness. I will be your loving friend as you are mine. Set me as a seal upon your heart, as the seal upon your hand, for love is stronger than death. And I will cherish you, honor you, uphold, and sustain you in all truth and sincerity. I will respect you and the divine image within you. I take you to be mine in love and tenderness. May my love for you last forever. May we be consecrated, one to the other, by these rings. Let our hearts be united in faith and hope, to beat as one in times of joy as in times of sorrow. Let our home be built on understanding and lovingkindness, rich with wisdom and reverence."

We are smiling.

"Blessed is the creation of the fruit of the vine," says Rachel, giving the secular version of the first of the traditional seven wedding blessings.

"Blessed is the creation which embodies glory.

"Blessed is the creation of the human being.

"Blessed is the design of the human being. We are assembled from the very fabric of the universe and are composed of eternal element. Blessed be and blessed is our creation.

"Rejoice and be glad, you who wandered homeless. In joy have you gathered with your sisters and your brothers. Blessed is the joy of our gathering.

"Bestow happiness on these two loving mates as would creatures feel in Eden's garden. Blessed be the joy of lovers.

"Blessed is the creation of joy and celebration, lover and mate, gladness and jubilation, pleasure and delight, love and solidarity, friendship and peace. Soon may we hear in the streets of the city and the paths of the fields the voice of joy, the voice of gladness, the voice of lover, the voice of mate, the triumphant voice of lovers from the canopy and the voice of youths from their feasts and song. Blessed, blessed, blessed is the joy of lovers, one with the other."

"We're coming to the end of the ceremony," says Rachel. "As we know, Mike and Joel legally married in Iowa. But their marriage wasn't complete; they needed this ceremony to make it whole. The completion of their marriage is us, their friends and family. The holy rituals we've enacted in this morning's ceremony solidify and strengthen their bond, but these rituals—along with our presence—also heal a little bit of the brokenness that they and so many others experience because of the injustice that still works in our lives.

"There's a legend that, when God created the world, He filled a collection of jars with light to help Him see what he was doing.

"But there was too much light, and the jars couldn't hold it all; they broke, and now the world is filled with the fragments of these shattered jars, light trapped in each one. As we go through life, it's our job as human beings to search for shards of these broken vessels and put them back together so that the light imprisoned in them can be released. In Hebrew this is called *tikkun ha'olam*—the healing of the world.

"Joel and Mike will now break a glass, reminding us of our duty to confront injustice wherever and in whatever form we find it and indicating that this wedding takes us one step further toward the healing of the world."

We move our feet next to each other over the light bulb wrapped in a napkin. ("You'd be surprised how hard it can be to break a glass," said Rachel when I objected to the substitution she suggested, to which Mike responded, "Joel has a special talent for it," but we followed her advice anyway.) When our feet are aligned, my size eights centered against his size elevens, we stomp down, shattering the light bulb.

We stand, unsure of what to do.

We look at each other.

We look around at our guests.

We look at each other again.

We start walking down the path out of the garden.

10

Living Happily Ever After

The party afterward was lovely. The sixty-odd wedding guests—some of them had taken it upon themselves to bring "plus one"s, and I could not find it in my heart to begrudge them— sat and stood around our backyard while our dogs wandered delightedly among them, Sasha playing the graceful *éminence grise* and Zoe licking the air as she does when she's truly happy.

Given the unspeakably early hour, the caterer wasn't finished preparing when we got back home, so people just mingled and conversed (and my father evidently told my friend Kirsten enough about the true story of Benedict Arnold that she immediately started writing a song about him) until the food was ready. Mike and I removed our top hats but this move met with monolithic disapproval on the part of our guests so we put them back on. The bartender from the bar down the street served mimosas, which I was told were delicious, and virgin orange fizzes, the deliciousness of which I experienced for myself.

The rule is that you're not allowed to leave a wedding party until the married couple leaves, which means that, if you're at the wedding of a particularly unaware couple who just can't stop celebrating, you end up trapped there, growing more bitter by the minute, until they finally depart and you can leave and start talking about the people you were sitting next to. None of the etiquette books I consulted, however, had any suggestions on how to handle the situation when the party was at the happy couple's home, so we decided that, when the time came, we'd just lock ourselves in our bedroom until everybody had left. I was therefore horrified when a couple of guests made their exit before we'd brought out the cupcakes, because it meant that they would forever remember the experience of my wedding as one marred by the absence of dessert; I would have resented them deeply for rendering my wedding imperfect in their future memories except I was already spending all my energy worrying that Mike and I were keeping our more etiquette-minded guests there against their will. Out came the cupcakes, then, and, though of course the lemon and red velvet cupcakes were inferior to the chocolate cupcakes, they were popular enough for me not to regret acceding to Mike's one-third / one-third / one-third proposal (but obviously some of our friends have disappointing taste, and I'm not sure what to do about that). We also had a small actual cake-cake which we cut and fed small pieces of to each other ("If you mash cake into my face," I'd said the night before, "I'm going to divorce you").

Then, as soon as we could, we locked ourselves in our bedroom, as per our plan, until all our guests left—I read and Mike napped—and before long we were on our way to the airport, our house keys in Mike's sister's hand so that she could clean up, return the double-crossing morning clothes, and take our exhausted dogs (licking that much air must take a lot of energy) to doggie sleepaway camp.

The trip to Miami was short, and after we boarded the ship the rest of the evening was like an evening on any other vacation—we engaged in the sorts of activities one engages in on one's wedding evening, to be sure, and they were particularly delightful, but the thing that struck me most, even disappointed me a little, was how *ordinary* it felt. I don't know what I'd been expecting: that I would start to sparkle like the vampires in *Twilight*, perhaps, or that I would actually be levitating a few inches off the ground? But those things didn't happen, because marriage isn't magic. It's about the relationship between a couple and society. It doesn't change anything within the couple, or within you.

The one wonderful difference was that eating dinner, just like grocery shopping on the day of the California Supreme Court's ruling in 2008, felt different. I looked around at the other passengers and saw a number of other presumably honeymooning couples. And I felt, to quote the Disney movie, part of their world. Not entirely—I mean, look at what they were wearing—but as I interrupted the waiter to ask him to stop telling me about the wine and just bring me a Diet Coke, as I pushed the potatoes to the side into a pile that I hoped would look like I had eaten some of them, as I savored (and wished the entire meal had been course after course of) the molten chocolate cake, I did so knowing that the commitment I had made to take care of my spouse was just as firm as theirs, just as deep, just as unshackled.

So I'm lying in a chair on the verandah off cabin 7199, Vista deck, of the Celebrity Millennium cruise ship as it sails toward Aruba.

I've never been on a cruise before, and now my only desire is to make enough money somehow never to have to get off this boat. For one thing, the verandah is covered, which means that I can sit here outside in the warm breeze with the smell of the sea all around me but not worry about getting second-degree burns like I did when my middle-school choir went to Miami Beach and I didn't realize that my sunblock wasn't waterproof. For another thing, between the hours of 7:00 a.m. and 2:00 a.m. there are exactly thirty minutes during which free food is not being hurled at me from a trebuchet. I also have with me several books I've bizarrely managed never to read, including *A Tale of Two Cities*, which by the way is *hilarious*, and if I run out there's a library on board that actually has a quarterway decent collection. The list of movies rentable on our TV is short and the menu corrects the spelling of *Inglorious Basterds*, but really what is that in the face of an inexhaustible supply of chocolate ice cream?

Over the last week and a half we've been to several Caribbean islands, including Grenada, where we ate lunch in a restaurant that served banana catsup as a condiment and had a big sign in front reading ABSOLUTELY NO BAREBACK PLEASE, and Dominica, where I accidentally went skinnydipping. But by far my favorite island, leaving Grenada and Dominica in the dust, has been Curaçao, because I went on a shore excursion there to the Dolphin Academy and swam with dolphins.

Mike had no interest whatsoever in swimming with dolphins, which I don't understand, and I mean really don't understand, not just fake don't understand so I can make a joke about it but really, like, why would anybody on earth not seize an opportunity to spend an afternoon playing with the puppies of the sea? But he wanted to take a tour of—I'm not making this up—island vegetation, so I went on my own.

And after the hour and a half I spent at the Dolphin Academy, I don't know how dolphins have refrained from taking over the earth.

The dolphins at the Dolphin Academy have been trained so that, if you reach out with both hands and tap the water on either side of you, a pair of them will come barreling toward you, catch your hands with their fins, and carry you like a shot to the end of the pool. If somebody tapped his hands on the water and expected *me* to come barreling toward him and catch his hand, he would be sorely disappointed, not because I'd refuse but because I'd *fail*. I'd run into the wall of the pool or end up grabbing his elbow or something. If you twirl your hands one way the dolphins will sing; twirl them the other way and they'll do back flips. These bastards are brilliant. Plus, the academy made us watch a movie about how terrible life is for most dolphins in captivity and then showed us all the measures they had taken to make things different at the Dolphin Academy. *And* one of the dolphins kissed me. All Mike got was stupid plants.

So now I'm lying, as I say, in a chair on the verandah off cabin 7199, Vista deck, of the Celebrity Millennium cruise ship as it sails toward Aruba. And I'm thinking, in the moments when I'm not wishing I could stay on this ship forever, about marriage equality. And, perhaps because I'm still in such a good mood from the dolphins, I have hope.

There are a few reasons for this. The first is that, as far as same-sexers are concerned, the story of America in the last century has been a tale of expanding freedom, and, despite the hideous direction the country has moved, in so many ways, over the last thirty years, I don't think there will be a true reversal in that expansion any time soon, because there are too many people keeping vigil too closely. And what this means is that same-sexers aren't going back into the closet. I suppose that, if the country is ever forced to pay for the greed of the plutocrats who have bought or at least rented its government, that may change—everything may collapse and social standards may all be turned on their heads and it will be a brave new world for everybody, with no iPhones or Lady Gaga or memory foam mattresses—but, barring that, the increase in liberty for same-sexers is going to continue in the foreseeable future. The people working against marriage equality are fighting a losing battle, and I suspect they know it.

But that's not the only reason I have hope for the future.

The night before the wedding, on CNN or ABC or whatever—at this point television news for me has two channels, Fox and Not Fox, and I can't stand to watch either one, because if it's on Not Fox it makes me so angry about what's going on in the world that I want to slit somebody's throat and if it's on Fox it makes me so angry about people lying about what's going on in the world that I want to slit somebody's throat twice—there was yet another tedious story about politicians' views on marriage equality. And there was a reporter at an anti-equality rally and she asked this guy why he didn't think gay people should be allowed to marry, and he said, "It just makes sense, marriage is about children. It's biological."

Well, I thought—and I assume most other same-sexers think something similar when confronted with this sort of rhetoric—*that's bullshit. If you actually thought that marriage was "about children," whatever that means, and that people who couldn't procreate shouldn't be permitted to marry, then you'd be saying that post-menopausal women shouldn't have the right to marry, you'd be saying*—I take this from Jonathan Rauch—*that if we allow men who've had vasectomies to marry we might as well allow bestiality and incest. The fact that you're not saying those things means that a belief that "marriage is about children" isn't the real reason you oppose marriage equality. The real reason you oppose marriage equality is that you just don't like us. The only reason you're saying anything about children is that you know it's socially unacceptable to* say *you don't like us.*

In other words, as far as I was concerned, not only did this guy oppose marriage equality because he didn't like same-sexers, but he was arguing in bad faith—he was saying something other than what he believed. What he truly thought was, *Faggots getting married—gross.* But he knew he wasn't really allowed to say that, so he had to come up with something else to say that would hide his bigotry from Not Fox News's audience. So in the end not only was he a bigot, he was also a liar. He wasn't interested in an honest discussion about the issue.

But I've been reading the work of a guy named Jonathan Haidt, a professor of psychology at the University of Virginia—like I said, the ship's library is a quarterway decent, plus there's the Internet—and I'm beginning to wonder whether things aren't maybe a little more complicated than that.

Several years ago, it seems, Haidt conducted an experiment in which he presented subjects with situations like the following: "Julie and Mark are a sister and brother vacationing in the south of France. They have some wine, one thing leads to another, and they decide they want to have sex. They use two different kinds of contraception and enjoy it, but they decide not to do it again. They find afterward that the experience has brought them closer together."

Haidt then asked his subjects whether what Julie and Mark did was wrong. In an interview with Tamler Sommers in *Believer Magazine*, Haidt says:

> People almost always start out by saying it's wrong. Then they start to give reasons. The most common reasons involve genetic abnormalities or that it will somehow damage their relationship. But we say in the story that they use two forms of birth control, and we say in the story that they keep that night as a special secret and that it makes them even closer. When the experimenter points out these facts and says, "Oh, well, sure, if they were going to have kids, that would cause problems, but they are using birth control, so would you say that it's OK?" And people never say "Ooooh, right, I forgot about the birth control. So then it *is* OK." Instead, they say, "Oh, yeah. Huh. Well, OK, let me think."
>
> So what's really clear, you can see it in the videotapes of the experiment, is: people give a reason. When that reason is stripped from them, they give another reason. When the new reason is stripped from them, they reach for *another* reason. And it's only when they reach deep into their pocket for another reason, and come up empty-handed, that they enter the state we call "moral dumbfounding." Because they fully expect to find reasons. They're *surprised* when they don't find reasons. And so in some of the videotapes you can see, they start laughing. But it's not an "it's so funny" laugh. It's more of a nervous-embarrassment puzzled laugh. So it's a cognitive state where you "know" that something is morally wrong, but you can't find reasons to justify your belief. Instead of changing your mind about what's wrong, you just say, "I don't know, I can't explain it. I just know it's wrong."

One of the conclusions Haidt draws from this is that moral reasoning is less "a judge searching for the truth" than "a lawyer trying to build a case. . . . The reasoning process constructs post-hoc justifications, yet we experience the illusion of objective reasoning."

As I read it, he's saying two things here:

The reasons we give for believing something aren't necessarily the real reasons we believe it.

We are unaware of that fact.

I think the implications of this are staggering.

Because if it's true, then it means that the guy on Not Fox News who says, "It just makes sense, marriage is about children" isn't dissembling, he's not attempting to hide any bigotry. He really does believe that his opposition to marriage equality comes from some notion having to do with procreation rather than from his disgust at the violation of a taboo. In other words: He may not like gay people, but he isn't necessarily arguing in bad faith. He may be a homophobe, but he may not know it. He's a bigot, but that doesn't mean he's a liar.

And what this means, ladies and germs, is that *his mind can be changed.*

Morgan Spurlock, best known as the director of *Supersize Me*, the documentary in which he ate nothing but food from McDonald's for a month and chronicled the appalling effects on his health, later created and hosted a television show (incredibly, on Fox) called *30 Days*, each episode of which plunged a volunteer into a community whose lifestyle he or she found abhorrent. A devout Baptist moved in with a Muslim family. A border-patrolling Minuteman lived with illegal immigrants. And in one episode, an ultra-conservative army reservist from Michigan spent a month as the roommate of a gay guy in the Castro, the gayest neighborhood in San Francisco.

When Ryan, attractive in a fresh, clean-cut, midwestern sort of way, arrives at Ed's apartment, he's obviously very uncomfortable and keeps saying things like, "As long as he doesn't touch me," and, though he's perfectly polite, is very clearly on his guard. Over the course of the month he relaxes, though the scenes in which they make him work in a super-gay wine and cheese store are never less than excruciating, not least because he can't pronounce the names of anything he's trying to sell. ("Bueno . . . bueno . . . gorno?" he says when asked to repeat the Italian for *hello*. "Buon jerno?" *Buon giorno*, his boss offers. "Guong jerno.") They send him to talk with Reverend Penny Nixon, head of San Francisco's Metropolitan Community Church, who asks some very smart questions but ultimately makes little headway with him. "To change my interpretation of the Bible," he says, "isn't something that somebody can tell me what they believe and have me believe differently." And it looks like the whole experience isn't going to make much of an impression on him.

And then he's talking to Ed after a visit to a gay chapter of the American Legion—this is three weeks or so into his month-long term—and he says, "I still keep my original opinion, that I don't feel comfortable with gays in the military."

And Ed says, "So if this war escalates and the draft starts up and I'm suddenly in your unit, how would that be?" And there's a pause.

"Wow," says Ryan finally. "That's a very interesting question, because it actually makes me contradict myself. I think actually— this is very weird to think about, because it wouldn't really bother me if you, specifically, were in my unit. I think you'd be a great soldier. I think that you could benefit the army. Yes, I'd be comfortable, you know, having you next to me."

It was an astonishing moment, something I'd never experienced before in my life: I actually *saw somebody's mind open on national television*.

Then, at a meeting of Parents and Friends of Lesbians and Gays (PFLAG), when a father talks about his hopes for his daughter, Ryan says, "I've been kind of one-sided about a lot of things. But being able to sit there and hear Sam say, with such love in his heart, that she should have all the same things, it's hard to say, I disagree with that. And if my brother or sister wanted to do that, I wouldn't be able to sit there and say, no, I don't think you should be able to do that."

"Why should my daughter be treated differently from her two brothers?" asks Sam.

"You're right," says Ryan. "She shouldn't." Then he sighs in frustration. "I have some thinking to do."

Now, I know better than most how little reality there can be in reality television, but in this case I think there was actually a great deal. I detected none of the awkward phrasings involved in parroting something the director has asked for, none of the weird intros that are the signs of answers to questions on Planet Reality. I'm sure Ryan and Ed spent an insane amount of time going through doors on Planet Again, and the narrative has been streamlined—hell, there's no such thing as narrative in real life; the narrative has been created—for TV, but I think that the month this guy spent in San Francisco really did change his mind about same-sexers.

And this is why I think we're ill served by things like the NOH8 campaign, for example, in which the wonderful photographer Adam Bouska has taken pictures of all sorts of celebrities with their mouths taped shut. Because sure, seeing Adam Lambert and Kathy Griffin and Cher with duct tape over their mouths is thrilling—how amazing to think that so many of our society's luminaries, plus the Kardashians, are willing to stand with us!— but I would be willing to bet a great deal of money that NOH8 didn't change very many people's minds. The episode of *30 Days* I've discussed aired in 2006, and Ryan didn't answer the Facebook message I sent him, so I have no idea how he feels about marriage equality now, but I'm confident that if today a guy with his background—we'll call him Brian—comes across a photo of Jane Lynch with duct tape over her mouth under a logo that says NOH8, he's going to dismiss it immediately.

Because Brian doesn't think he hates gay people. And so from his perspective a sign that says NOH8 is at best made-up nonsense and at worst a lie.

About three-quarters of the way through the 1999 movie *The Talented Mr. Ripley* comes a monologue in which Matt Damon says, "Whatever you do, however terrible, however hurtful—it all makes sense, doesn't it? In your head. You never meet anybody who thinks they're a bad person." (In the book on which the movie is based, his character is nowhere near as charmingly naïve, but that's neither here nor there.) And, though I doubt that most people who vote against marriage equality are actually lunatic killers, as Matt Damon turns out to be in *The Talented Mr. Ripley*, I still think same-sexers have to understand the truth of what he says if we're ever going to change the way people see us.

It's like when we hear people at a demonstration yelling about how same-sexers want to destroy the family. We think they're stupid, or insane, or lying. Because we know that whatever changes we want to make to the institution of marriage as America knows it are not to destroy the family but to strengthen it.

But they don't.

To the people yelling, what we're doing looks a hell of a lot like an attempt to destroy the family.

Just like what they're doing looks a hell of a lot like hatred to us.

Let me be clear that I'm not talking about the politicians, most of whom I think are lying sociopaths far more dangerous than the talented Mr. Ripley. When Mitt Romney or Newt Gingrich or John Boehner says "Marriage is about procreation," I'm certain he knows perfectly well that isn't what he thinks. (I'm actually certain Mitt Romney, Newt Gingrich, and John Boehner don't give a damn about marriage equality one way or another, and they're just saying what they know will get them votes.) So none of what I'm talking about, unfortunately, applies to the people who are actually running things. But the rest of the country—real America—I believe they can be reached.

And so I think it's far, far too easy to march around with signs that say, "Hate is not a family value," shouting about hate this and hate that and hate the other thing and not letting people get past the word "Jesus" before we glitter-bomb them. Doing so feels great, because after all the crap that's been hurled at us for years, decades, centuries, millennia, hurling some of it back is extraordinarily liberating.

But it also lets them—and us—off the hook. It allows us to avoid the hard work of actual dialogue. I don't mean you-think-one-thing-and-I-think-another-so-let's-find-a-way-to-agree-to-disagree dialogue, because that's not enough; agreeing to disagree about whether same-sexers deserve equal treatment under the law would be a pretty pathetic resolution. I mean working to help them see things from our perspective, which requires first working to see things from theirs.

As to how we go about doing so—well, I don't know. I do know that research by Gregory M. Herek shows that it takes, on average, two positive interactions of some depth with a same-sexer for a homophobe to change his or her mind. Maybe part of the answer involves having as many of these interactions with as many people as we can. If I could figure out how to drop every bigot in the country into the house or apartment of a same-sexer for a month so a whole lot of people could turn a whole lot of *thems* into *us*-es, I'd be doing that instead of writing this book. Sure, some people's minds are less open than others' to begin with, and sure, there are people, not even sociopaths but regular people, who will be unable to change the way they think, just like there are same-sexers who are unable to change the way we think about whatever group we think of as "them" in any given moment, people of color, devout Christians, effeminate gay men, whoever. But I don't believe it's beyond human ken to understand that we and the people we see as our enemies are the same, and that in this matter we all want exactly the same thing.

Now, if you'll excuse me, there's chocolate ice cream calling my name.

Epilogue

It's October of 2012, and as Mike and I are now coming up on our two-year anniversary it seemed appropriate to tie up a few loose ends.

I did not win the HGTV Urban Oasis Giveaway, even though I stayed up all night the night before the wedding writing entry cards and addressing envelopes and filled up both our neighborhood mailboxes so completely on the way to the airport that there was no room left in them and I had to send like five hundred of the entries from Puerto Rico. In the end the contest had fifteen and a half million entries, which means that by filling out and sending all those index cards along with entering online every day I increased my chances of winning an apartment in the Residences at the W Hotel, if my math is correct, from 1 in 256,410 to 1 in 3,846. Fortune chose not to smile upon me, however, and the apartment went to some college kid in Florida who claimed to have entered only once. I'm not sorry to have made the attempt, though; it makes me feel like I haven't completely lost the ability to tilt at windmills.

Apple juice, I discovered not long after the wedding, is a perfectly acceptable substitute for wine according to even the strictest interpretations of Jewish law, so there are no problems there and I can still think of the Japanese Hill and Pond Garden as Eden.

After our Brooklyn wedding ceremony, unlike after our ceremony in Iowa, I do feel married. I call Mike my husband and feel that I'm telling the truth. I don't know that I would feel the same way if I lived in a state whose laws, unlike those of New York, didn't recognize marriages of same-sex couples, but, for better and for worse, I don't really have any way of finding out, because the answer sure as hell isn't interesting enough to be worth moving back to South Carolina.

Our long string of not suffering as a result of marriage inequality was finally broken a few months ago, when the IRS sent Mike a letter telling him he owed $16,000 more in taxes than he'd paid.

"Oh, my God, honey!" I said, full of excitement, when I understood why they wanted what they wanted. "We're being discriminated against because we're gay married!"

(My excitement might have cooled significantly had a few phone calls not cleared the issue up, but they did. There are a lot of same-sexers, however, who are not in a position to joke about things like this.)

The day after we got back from the honeymoon I walked into the kitchen with a bag of groceries. After I had taken the pasta and the vegetables out, after I'd put the dairy away, after I'd eaten less of the ice cream than I wanted to because I knew Mike would be annoyed that I'd eaten any but if I left a lot then he would get over it more quickly, I went to the stove and reached up to get a pot to boil the water in.

And there, sitting on the shelf, were the pot and pan lids that had been missing since I dragged them into the basement along with everything else in the kitchen years before. They shone as brightly as they had the day I bought them.

"Where did you find the pot and pan lids?" I asked Cathy on the phone as I chopped a tomato.

"What are you talking about?"

"Our pot and pan lids have been missing for years, but you obviously found them when you cleaned up after the party and put them back with the pots and pans. Where were they?"

"Joel, I didn't find any pot or pan lids."

"But you must have, because here they are."

"Are you sure you didn't get too much sun in the Caribbean?"

When Mike came down for dinner, I asked him, and he had no idea where they had come from either. "Maybe we should call your mom," I said, "and get her to ask 28 what he thinks."

"No, because he'll just say they were where they needed to be."

"And then yell at us for not talking to him in so long."

All I can think, really, is that the pot and pan lids had lain in wait for years until they could return as some sort of metaphor about marriage or completion or healing.

Or maybe they just appeared when we were ready for them.

Appendix

A Brief and Highly Biased Legislative History of American Marriage Equality with Respect to Sexuality

The first marriage of a same-sex couple in the United States, I was surprised to learn when I started doing research about the question, took place not in 2004 in Massachusetts or California, nor in 2000 in Vermont, but in 1971 in Minnesota, when Michael McConnell and Jack Baker plighted their troth, marriage license, wide lapels, and all. McConnell and Baker, who was president of the first gay student organization in the United States (FREE, "Fight Repression of Erotic Expression," formed a month before the Stonewall riots in New York City catalyzed the gay rights movement) and also president of the University of Minnesota's student body (his campaign poster, which showed him in jeans and high heels, read, "Put yourself in Jack Baker's shoes"), were denied a marriage license in Hennepin County and, after filing suit in the state Supreme Court, skipped, well, gaily over to Blue Earth County, where they were issued a license. Eventually the Minnesota District Court ruled that Hennepin County was correct not to issue McConnell and Baker a marriage license, but nobody ever said or did anything about Blue Earth County, so as far as I'm concerned McConnell and Baker are legally husband and husband.

When they celebrated their nuptials, however, I was not yet a twinkle in my mother's eye, and when a few couples in Colorado followed in their footsteps in 1975 ("You have failed to establish," read the government's letter to one, "that a bona fide marital relationship can exist between two faggots"), I had yet to learn the alphabet. The marriage equality movement as I know it began on May 5, 1993, when the Hawai'i Supreme Court ruled that the state might not have a constitutional right to forbid same-sex couples to marry. The citizens of Hawai'i at once took brisk and efficient care of this by amending their constitution so that the state definitely had a constitutional right to forbid same-sex couples to marry, but at this point I had never been on more than two dates with a man, not counting that twenty-three-year-old Seth I'd sort of half-dated in high school, and given the fact that while we were making out on our third date I burst a zit and got pimple gunk all over his face, not to mention the fact that I guess he was my statutory rapist, it's probably best not to count him anyway; while I was naturally dismayed at the change in Hawai'i's constitution, therefore, that dismay was greater in principle than in practice.

Six years later the Vermont Supreme Court held that excluding same-sex couples from the benefits and protections incident to marriage under state law was unconstitutional. The Vermont state legislature took brisk and efficient care of this by creating something called a civil union, a new status designed to include same-sex couples in all the benefits and protections incident to marriage under state law. This wasn't marriage, but it seemed pretty damn close (though it became clear before long that the benefits and protections incident to marriage under state law in which same-sex couples were included meant everything except any of the benefits and protections incident to marriage under state law). By this time I had been on more than two dates with exactly one man, though given the pants he wore on our fourth date I suppose it's best not to count him, either.

Before long Ontario had thrown its hat into the ring by allowing same-sex couples to get *married* married, followed swiftly by other Canadian provinces. While, having just broken up with a guy who'd named a cat Beautiful Music, I had at the time no desire to get married, I still took a theoretical interest in the subject (actually, he'd broken up with me, but how embarrassing is it to admit that one has been dumped by a guy who named a cat Beautiful Music?). But I saw two problems with the idea of getting married in Canada. First, after poking around I discovered that, while apparently all you need to get married in Canada is vertebrae, if two people married in Canada want to get *divorced* at least one of them has to have lived there for at least twelve months. I think Montréal is great and all, but my heart did not leap at the thought of spending a year of my life in a country where milk comes in bags. (Of course any marriage I contracted would be indestructible and so I would never need to worry about divorce, but I was working on the better-safe-than-sorry principle.)

More important, though, I didn't want to get married in another country, because I wanted to stand on unshakable ground when it came to the Constitution of the United States. I don't particularly wish to end up before the Supreme Court, but I can imagine a situation in which Associate Justice Antonin Scalia— may his eyes be put out with a carving fork only to regenerate immediately so that they can be put out again from day to day to the last syllable of recorded time—decided that the Constitution didn't require the United States to recognize marriages of same-sex couples performed in another country, and I can imagine a compelling (if repugnant) argument being made to support such a decision. No; if Associate Justice Antonin Scalia—may his skin be peeled off layer by excruciating layer while he is doused repeatedly with salt-laced moonshine—was going to deny me the right to marry, his ruling was going to be so clearly unconstitutional that future historians would be able to look upon it only as an indication of how absolutely batshit crazy those third-millennium savages were.

Heterosexual-only marriage fell to the sword next in Massachusetts, whose Supreme Court finally went all the way in 2004 and said same-sexers had to be allowed to marry, no "benefits and protections" or "state compelling interest" about it. As I hadn't stopped reeling yet from the Beautiful-Music guy, my view was still academic, but I was nevertheless excited about the potential future I could imagine in which I was not insane enough to date somebody who would own a cat to begin with—excited, that is, until then-Governor Mitt Romney started digging through state congressional archives and found Massachusetts General Laws Chapter 207, Section 11, otherwise known as the Marriage Evasion Act; passed in 1913, it forbade out-of-state couples to marry in Massachusetts if their marriage wouldn't be considered valid in their home state. This seems an odd action to find so problematic as to prohibit by law, until one discovers that in 1913 nationally renowned boxer Jack Johnson, who was black, had just married Lucille Cameron, who was white, thereby throwing the United States into an epic battle over the evils of interracial marriage, or, as they called it back then, "miscegenation" or "amalgamation." The Massachusetts law was designed to prevent a flood of out-of-state mixed-race couples from going to Massachusetts, getting legally married there, going back to their home states, and drowning American decency in their miscegenated filth. (This was a time, remember, when if seven of your great-grandparents had been white and one had been black you were known as an octoroon and trying to eat at a white restaurant meant that before the evening was through you would end up hanging from a tree.)

In the twenty-first century, miscegenation having been permitted for decades and American decency having survived somehow all the same, bloody perhaps but unbowed, I guess people had forgotten about the Marriage Evasion Act. But when Governor Romney, nothing if not an effective husbander of re-sources, realized he could use it to prevent out-of-state same-sex couples from going to Massachusetts, getting legally married there, going back to their home states, and drowning American decency in their homosexual filth, he took it out of storage, dusted it off, and gave it pride of place on the mantelpiece again. And now the only way same-sexers who lived outside of Massachusetts could get married there was to move to one of the states in which same-sex couples weren't expressly forbidden to marry—a group that before long consisted of only Rhode Island. On August 31, 2007, there were also four hours during which same-sexers in Iowa could legally obtain marriage licenses, but the judge who rendered that decision immediately issued a stay of his judgment until the whole thing could be sorted out, which I appreciated at the time, because otherwise I *knew* Mike would have had me on the next plane to Cedar Rapids, and in the end only two gay couples got married in Iowa that year.

Which brings us to the beginning of chapter one.

Acknowledgments

My first thanks, as usual, must go to Joy Tutela, still the sexiest agent in America, David Black, still the second-sexiest agent in America, Raphael Kadushin, the sexiest editor in America, and Matthew Cosby, Saryta Rodriguez, and Luke Thomas, the sexiest assistants in America.

Without Sarah Rose I wouldn't even have been able to have the idea in the first place, much less execute it in anything like an interesting way.

The many friends who read bits and pieces large and small already know how much I appreciated their feedback, but it's worth saying again. I highly recommend Nancy Rawlinson (nancyrawlinson.com) and Anne Mini (annemini.com) if anybody's looking to work with a freelance editor; without the advice they gave me, along with that of Victoria Cain, Kirsten Childs, my brother, Jeremy, Chris Hampton, Leonard Jacobs, and Julia Sullivan, I'd have been lucky to dig half as deep as I did. Ted Kadin both kept my Talmudic interpretations from going too far off track and is a fantastic calligrapher (tedkadin.com).

Dr. Kleinbaum kept me sane.

And Mike forgave me.

Any mistakes are the fault of Charles and David Koch.

LIVING OUT

Gay and Lesbian Autobiographies

David Bergman, Joan Larkin, and Raphael Kadushin
SERIES EDITORS

Two Novels: "Development" and "Two Selves"
Bryher

The Hurry-Up Song: A Memoir of Losing My Brother
Clifford Chase

In My Father's Arms: A Son's Story of Sexual Abuse
Walter A. de Milly III

Lawfully Wedded Husband: How My Gay Marriage Will Save
    the American Family
Joel Derfner

Midlife Queer: Autobiography of a Decade, 1971–1981
Martin Duberman

The Man Who Would Marry Susan Sontag: And Other Intimate
    Literary Portraits of the Bohemian Era
Edward Field

Body, Remember: A Memoir
Kenny Fries

Travels in a Gay Nation: Portraits of LGBTQ Americans
Philip Gambone

Autobiography of My Hungers
Rigoberto González

Widescreen Dreams: Growing Up Gay at the Movies
Patrick E. Horrigan

The End of Being Known: A Memoir
Michael Klein